AQA PSYCHOLOGY

FOR A LEVEL
YEAR 1 & AS

Cara Flanagan

Dave Berry

Michael Griffin

Rob Liddle

Revision Guide

Illuminate
Publishing

Published in 2016 by Illuminate Publishing Ltd,
P.O. Box 1160, Cheltenham, Gloucestershire GL50 9RW
Orders: Please visit www.illuminatepublishing.com
or email sales@illuminatepublishing.com

British Library Cataloguing in Publication Data
A catalogue record for this book is available from the
British Library

ISBN 978-1-908682-44-4

Printed by Cambrian Printers, Aberystwyth

11.16

The publisher's policy is to use papers that are natural,
renewable and recyclable products made from
wood grown in sustainable forests. The logging and
manufacturing processes are expected to conform to the
environmental regulations of the country of origin.

Every effort has been made to contact copyright holders
of material produced in this book. If notifed, the publisher
will be pleased to rectify any errors or omissions at the
earliest opportunity.

Editor: Geoff Tuttle

Cover design: Nigel Harriss

Text design: Nigel Harriss and John Dickinson

Layout: John Dickinson

Front cover photographer: Julia Trotti

Model: Madeline Rae Mason

Makeup: Lidija Jevremovic

Stylist: Jessie McNaught

Acknowledgements:

p.12, 16, 18, 32, 36, 38, 44, 90, 96, 115, 122 © Illuminate Publishing

p.73 © Craig Swanson www.perspicuity.com:

p.3 and 128 stars Aha-Soft / Shutterstock.com; p.5 marekuliasz /
Shutterstock.com; Aleksova / Shutterstock.com; Sashkin / Shutterstock.
com; p.6 Kuklos / Shutterstock.com; p.7 ostill / Shutterstock.com;
p.10 Baronb / Shutterstock.com; p.11 lexaarts / Shutterstock.com;
p.13 Stokkete / Shutterstock.com; p.14 Fer Gregory / Shutterstock.
com; p.15 bikeriderlondon / Shutterstock.com; p.16 style-photography
/ Shutterstock.com; p.17 alphaspirit / Shutterstock.com; p.18 Elnur /
Shutterstock.com; p.19 bikeriderlondon / Shutterstock.com; p.20 Sergey
Nivens / Shutterstock.com; p.21 Iakov Filimonov / Shutterstock.com;
p.22 Quick Shot / Shutterstock.com; p.23 BlueSkyImage / Shutterstock.
com; p.24 Nikita Vishneveckiy / Shutterstock.com; p.26 Pixeljoy /
Shutterstock.com; p.27 Peter Gudella / Shutterstock.com;
p.28 seahorsetwo / Shutterstock.com; p.29 Both stockphoto-graf /
Shutterstock.com; p.30 Max Bukovski / Shutterstock.com; p.32 Frank
Gaertner / Shutterstock.com; p.33 Anelina / Shutterstock.com;
p.34 ra2studio / Shutterstock.com; p.35 Kotin / Shutterstock.com;
p.37 alphaspirit / Shutterstock.com; p.38 SFC / Shutterstock.com;
p.39 Ollyy; p.40 ER_09 / Shutterstock.com; MaryValery / Shutterstock.
com; p.41 Jesada Sabai / Shutterstock.com; p.42 Igorusha /
Shutterstock.com; p.43 CREATISTA / Shutterstock.com;
p.45 wickerwood / Shutterstock.com; p.46 Brian A Jackson /
Shutterstock.com; p.47 Photographee.eu / Shutterstock.com;
p.48 Monkey Business Images; p.49 Viktor Gladkov; p.50 Olesia Bilkei
/ Shutterstock.com; fotofeel / Shutterstock.com; p.52 Liquorice Legs /
Shutterstock.com; p.53 Olga Maer / Shutterstock.com; p.54 Tinseltown
/ Shutterstock.com; SCIENCE SOURCE/SCIENCE PHOTO LIBRARY;
kathmanduphotog / Shutterstock.com; p.56 gresei / Shutterstock.com;
p.57 Olinchuk / Shutterstock.com; p.58 RimDream / Shutterstock.com;
p.59 VGstockstudio / Shutterstock.com; p.60 Rasulov / Shutterstock.
com; p.61 Monkey Business Images / Shutterstock.com; p.62 Feel Photo
Art / Shutterstock.com; p.63 Sarah Noda / Shutterstock.com;
p.64 Cheryl Casey / Shutterstock.com; p.65 adriaticfoto / Shutterstock.
com; p.66 Radiokafka / Shutterstock.com; p.67 ChiccoDodiFC /
Shutterstock.com; p.68 Syda Productions / Shutterstock.com;
p.69 Kaspars Grinvalds / Shutterstock.com; p.70 CYCLONEPROJECT /
Shutterstock.com; p.72 WilleeCole Photography / Shutterstock.com;
p.74 Evgeny Atamanenko / Shutterstock.com; p.77 Lukiyanova Natalia /
frenta / Shutterstock.com; p.78 Katrina Elena / Shutterstock.com;
p.79 klss / Shutterstock.com; p.81 Mike Baldwin / Cornered; p.82 Fotolia;
p.83 joshya / Shutterstock.com; p.84 RACOBOVT / Shutterstock.com;
p.85 ehmi nanthis / Shutterstock.com; p.86 Joseph Sohm / Shutterstock.
com; p.87 Jane0606 / Shutterstock.com; p.88 arda savasciogullari /
Shutterstock.com; p.89 gielmichal / Shutterstock.com; p.90 Lightspring /
Shutterstock.com; p.92 yochika photographer / Shutterstock.com;
p.93 Brocreative / Shutterstock.com; p.94 bikeriderlondon / Shutterstock.
com; p.97 Photographee.eu / Shutterstock.com; p.98 Zastolskiy Victor /
Shutterstock.com; p.99 PathDoc / Shutterstock.com; p.100 Twin Design
/ Shutterstock.com; p.101 Aaron Amat / Shutterstock.com; p.102 SoRad
/ Shutterstock.com; p.103 rdrgraphe / Shutterstock.com; p.104 MJTH
/ Shutterstock.com; p.105 Guayo Fuentes / Shutterstock.com; Marcos
Mesa Sam Wordley / Shutterstock.com; Moustache Girl / Shutterstock.
com; p.106 pirke / Shutterstock.com; p.107 Melica / Shutterstock.
com; p.109 Vitalinka / Shutterstock.com; p.110 Stefano Cavoretto /
Shutterstock.com; p.111 BeRad / Shutterstock.com; p.112 Anna.zabella /
Shutterstock.com; p.113 PathDoc / Shutterstock.com; p.115 THPStock /
Shutterstock.com; p.116 John T Takai / Shutterstock.com;
p.117 Kjpargeter / Shutterstock.com; p.118 g-stockstudio / Shutterstock.
com; p.120 Iakov Kalinin / Shutterstock.com.

Unsung heroes

This wonderful little book is the product of
the four authors (who also produced THE
APP) but we owe considerable gratitude
to our friend and writing partner Matt
Jarvis for sharing his material, to Arwa
Mohamedbhai for writing the suggested
answers to the Knowledge Check feature
(see p6 for details) and above all those who
manage the whole production – first of all
our mentor and publisher, Rick Jackman
and his team at Illuminate (Clare Jackman,
Peter Burton and Saskia Santos).

Second to the Nigemeister – Nigel Harriss,
supreme designer who is responsible for
the unique and spectacular design. He has
been assisted in the design and layout of
the book by John Dickinson.

And finally to Geoff Tuttle who dots all the
I's and a lot more in ensuring the beauty of
our words. Thank you.

About the authors

Cara is author of many books for A level students and a conference
organiser and speaker; she is also senior editor of *Psychology Review*. She
is looking forward to spending more time lying on a beach or climbing
mountains.

Dave is a co-author of *AQA Psychology for AS and Year 1 A Level*
by Illuminate Publishing, Dave is a full-time psychology teacher and
experienced examiner. He has led many face-to-face and on-line training
sessions for teachers and is looking forward to his next sleep.

Mike is a teacher of psychology, Assistant Headteacher and previous
Head of Sixth Form. He is an author of resources for the delivery of
psychology lessons and provides CPD for other psychology teachers. He is
enjoying being a new Daddy and looking forward to spending more time
changing nappies.

Rob was an A level psychology teacher for more than 20 years, before
turning to writing. He's also taught undergraduates. Rob's been told
often enough (by his wife, mainly) that he's a bit of a geek. It's true that
he likes nothing more than to settle down of an evening with a big book
of facts. He still buys CDs, and will explain why at great length unless
someone stops him. He still hasn't seen *Frozen*, despite having two
grand-daughters.

CONTENTS

Need extra revision power?

AQA PSYCHOLOGY FOR A LEVEL YEAR 1 & AS

Revision Guide

CARA FLANAGAN
DAVE BERRY
MIKE GRIFFIN
ROB LIDDLE

Illuminate Publishing

AQA A LEVEL PSYCHOLOGY

This wonderful Revision Guide will make your revision fly. Combine it with the accompanying *Revision App* and boost your revision into the stratosphere!

See back page for details

Introduction

Exam advice

AO stands for 'assessment objective'.

The 'Apply it' questions throughout this book aim to help you practise AO2 skills; 30% of the marks in the exam are AO2.

The exam papers are divided into sections (Section A, Section B, etc).

In Section A on paper 1 there are questions on Social Influence and Section B is on Memory – but the *type* of question is unpredictable. You might have an essay question and/or there may be research methods questions and/or an application question. There is no pattern to the way the types of questions are distributed on the exam.

Research methods questions will be in every section in addition to the Research Methods section on Paper 2.

25%

At least 25% of the marks for your AS exam will come from questions on research methods.

Type of exam questions

AO1	Define, outline, describe, explain	Explain what is meant by 'obedience'. (2 marks)
		Outline **one** emotional characteristic of depression. (2 marks)
		Explain what 'modelling' in relation to social learning theory means. Illustrate your answer with an example. (4 marks)
AO2	Application	[Stem] Tulisa has started at a new school and notices that all the girls are wearing long skirts. She doesn't want to be different and wants them to like her, so the next day she wears a long skirt, too.
		[Question] Explain which type of conformity Tulisa is showing. Explain your decision. (3 marks)
AO3	One criticism	Outline **one** criticism of the multi-store model. (2 marks)
	Evaluation	Evaluate Bowlby's monotropic theory of attachment. (6 marks)
AO1 + AO3	Mini-essays	Discuss research into conformity. (8 marks)
	Extended writing	Outline and evaluate a dispositional explanation for obedience. (12 marks AS, 16 marks AL)
		Describe and evaluate Romanian orphan studies. (12 marks AS, 16 marks AL)
AO1 + AO2 + AO3	Extended writing + applications	[Stem] Maria recently failed her driving test. She says the test was unfair and the examiner was 'out to get her'. She says she hates herself and will never try anything again. Before the test Maria told her friend that she had to pass otherwise she could not go on. Maria's friend thinks she might be showing signs of depression.
		[Question] Describe and evaluate the cognitive approach to explaining depression. Refer to Maria in your answer. (12 marks AS, 16 marks AL)

Research methods questions

AO1	Explain	Explain what is meant by a 'behavioural category'. (2 marks)
AO2	Application	[Stem] Participants were given a list of organised and unorganised words and their recall was tested.
		[Question] Explain how randomisation could have been used in this experiment. (2 marks)
AO3	Evaluate	Explain **one** strength of an independent groups design. (2 marks)

What to do for a Grade A

Top class AO1	Top class AO1 … includes details and specialist terms. For example: • This is good → Milgram (in the 1960s) described the agentic state as an explanation … • This isn't good → One study found people obeyed someone who was in charge… You don't need to write more, you just need to include specific bits of information such as specialist terms, researcher's names, percentages and so on.
Top class AO2	Top class AO2 … uses text or quotes from the stem of the question. For example: • This is good → Tulisa is showing normative social influence because she wears a long skirt so she is like the others and they will like her. • This isn't good → One type of conformity is normative which is wanting to be liked, like Tulisa. It's not enough to just mention a few key words – you must really engage with the stem. This is a skill that needs practice.

Top class AO3	Top class AO3 … is elaborated and therefore effective.. For example:
	❶ *Beginner* level: State your point: One criticism is … This theory is supported by … One strength is ….
	❷ *Intermediate* level: Add some *context*.
	  • This is good → One limitation is that artificial materials were used. The study by the Petersons used consonant syllables.
	  • This isn't good → One limitation is that artificial materials were used. This doesn't tell us about everyday life.
	  The second example is generic – it could be used anywhere.
	  Context is king.
	❸ *Expert* level: Add further explanation to make the point *thorough* + finish 'This shows that …'
	  Read the criticisms throughout this book as examples of expert level.
	
	If you find expert level difficult then just do intermediate. In an essay do five intermediate criticisms and that should get you the full 6 marks for AS.
	Whatever you do AVOID a list of beginner level criticisms with no context.

Top class AS essays	Make it organised – it helps the examiner see the separate elements of your answer. Use paragraphs. There is more advice on essay (extended writing) questions on the next page …

Describe **FEWER** studies but describe them in detail.

Identify **FEWER** critical points, but explain each one thoroughly.

ALL I WANT FOR CHRISTMAS

List-like is bad.

It's actually quite easy to list lots of points – explaining them is challenging.

Context is king

Good evaluation points must contain evidence.

Your point may be well-elaborated but, if the same elaborated point can be placed in many different essays then it is too **EASY**.

Good evaluation points must have **CONTEXT**.

Exam advice

The term 'research' refers to theories, explanations or studies.

KNOWLEDGE CHECK

The questions throughout this book should help you identify all the different ways that questions can be asked.

On the AS paper there are 72 marks and it is a 90-minute exam, which gives you 1¼ minutes for each mark.

On A level papers there are 96 marks and it is a 120-minute exam which also gives you 1¼ minutes for each mark.

Just because you have written lots doesn't mean you will get high marks.

Students who write long answers often do poorly.

- It may not answer the question.
- Spending too much time on one question means less time elsewhere.
- Your answer may lack detail – lists of studies and lists of critical points don't get high marks.
- Long essays are often very descriptive and there are never more than 6 marks for description.

Download suggested answers to the Knowledge Check questions from **tinyurl.com/jfds52r**

More information if you can bear it

There are lots of little rules

One or more Two or more	*Describe **one or more** explanations of obedience.* (10 marks) Means you can potentially gain full marks for just one explanation (gives you time to describe and evaluate it fully, which is important to show detail). Or you can elect to do more explanations – but too many explanations is not good because your answer becomes list-like (no details).
Distinguish between	*Distinguish between insecure–resistant and insecure–avoidant attachment types.* (4 marks) The danger is that you will simply describe each item. You must find a way to contrast them both, for example considering how each attachment type responds to stranger anxiety.
Essays with extra information	*Discuss the behaviourist approach. Refer to evidence in your answers.* (12 marks) *Describe **one** animal study of attachment. Include details of what the researcher(s) did and what they found.* (4 marks) Make sure you satisfy the demands of ALL parts of the question.

How much should I write?

In general 25–30 words per mark is a good rule – as long as the answer is focused on the topic.

For an AS essay of 12 marks you might therefore write:

    AO1 150–200 words   AO3 150–200 words

For an AL essay of 16 marks you might therefore write:

    AO1 150–200 words   AO3 250–300 words

Here are two ways to produce top class AS essays:

Route 1	**Route 2**
6 marks AO1	*6 marks AO1*
Six paragraphs/points, write about 150 words.	*Six* paragraphs/points, write about 150 words.
6 marks AO3	*6 marks AO3*
Five paragraphs/criticisms at *intermediate level.*	*Three* paragraphs/criticisms at *expert level.* Doing just three gives you time to elaborate more.

Effective revision

Create revision cards	For description the maximum you need is about 150 words.

- Identify 6–8 points on the topic.
- Record a trigger phrase in left hand column.
- Record about 25–30 words in right hand column.

For example

AO1 Key point	Description
Locus of control (LOC)	Rotter suggested people have a sense of what controls their behaviour.
Internals	Some people believe that the things that happen to them are largely controlled by themselves. For example, if you do well in an exam it is because you worked hard.
Externals	Other people believe that things happen without their control. If they did well in an exam they might say it iwas good luck or the textbook. If they fail it was bad luck or the questions were hard.

Reduce your cards to the minimum

Cue words	Description
Rotter LOC	A sense of what controls your behaviour.
Internal	Own control, e.g. poor exam mark due to lack of effort.
External	Outside our control, e.g. bad luck, bad teacher.

For the evaluation the maximum you need is about 150 words.

- Identify 3–5 critical points.
- Record a trigger phrase in left-hand column.
- Record context in the next column.
- If you are doing expert level add a further column or two further columns (as we have in this book).

For example

AO3 Key point	Intermediate level evaluation	Expert level evaluation
There is research support	Holland measured levels of LOC in a repeat of Milgram's study and found that more internals resisted the order to continue to the end than externals.	This supports the link between LOC and resistance to obedience. It is a valid explanation.

Rehearse the trigger phrases	Cover up the right-hand column and try to recall what is there using the trigger phrase.
Rehearse the content	When you are standing at a bus stop, see if you can remember all the trigger words for one topic.
Practise writing timed answers	Write an essay answer with your trigger card in front of you. Give yourself 15 minutes for a 12-mark answer. Give yourself 20 minutes for a 16-mark answer.

If you learn too much you will just try to squeeze it into the exam and you don't have time.

Focus on fewer points and make sure you explain them in detail. That's where the marks are.

in this book we have aimed to provide 6–8 points of AO1 for each topic, consisting of a trigger word and explanations. For example on page 32 you will find the following AO1 (descriptive) content:

Separate memory stores.	The MSM describes how information flows through the memory system. Memory is made of three stores linked by processing.
Sensory register (SR)	A stimulus from the environment (e.g. the sound of someone talking) passes into the SR along with lots of other sights, sounds, etc. This part of memory is not one store but five, one for each sense. • Duration: very brief – less than half a second. • Capacity: high, e.g. over one hundred million cells in one eye, each storing data. • Coding: depends on the sense – visual, auditory, etc.
Transfer from SR to STM	Little of what goes into the SR passes further into the memory system – needs attention to be paid to it.
Short-term memory (STM)	STM is a limited capacity and duration store. • Duration: about 18 to 30 seconds unless the information is rehearsed. • Capacity: between 5 and 9 items before some forgetting occurs. • Coding: acoustic.
Transfer from STM to LTM	*Maintenance rehearsal* occurs when we repeat (rehearse) material to ourselves. We can keep information in STM as long as we rehearse it. If we rehearse it long enough, it passes into LTM.
Long-term memory (LTM)	A permanent memory store When we want to recall materials stored in LTM it has to be transferred back to STM by a process called retrieval. • Duration: potentially up to a lifetime. • Capacity: potentially unlimited. • Coding: tends to be in terms of meaning, i.e. semantic.

No athlete would dream of running a race without doing many practice runs of the right distance and within a set time.

Understanding marking

AO1 question: Outline the procedure used in one study of animal attachment. (4 marks)

Answer Harlow's study was with baby monkeys. He had observed that baby monkeys often survived better in cages without their mother if you gave them a soft cloth to cuddle. He set up an experiment to test this where there were two wire mothers. One of the mothers had a feeding bottle attached while the other one was covered in cloth. The monkeys were kept all the time in a cage just with these two wire mothers. The monkeys spent their time with the cloth-covered mother not the other one, which shows that contact comfort is important in attachment.

AO2 question: Some friends are planning what they might do at the weekend. Most of them want to try out a new nightclub. But Sam fancies going to see a band he likes instead.

Briefly explain how each of the factors of group size, unanimity and task difficulty might influence whether or not Sam conforms to the majority. (6 marks)

Answer Sam is likely to conform if more than three of his friends want to go to the new club. Asch found, in his research, that levels of conformity rose up to having three confederates but it didn't get more after that. So a majority of three is probably enough – but in Asch's research that led to 32% conformity so Sam might still not conform.

If one of his friends decided not to go then Sam might feel more likely to dissent too. Asch found that even if the dissenter gave a different answer from the real participant this was enough to break the conformity. So Sam might go to see the band even if the dissenting friend wasn't going to do that either.

In terms of task difficulty it sounds like the band is something he knows well (a band he likes) whereas the nightclub is new and a less safe option which might make Sam more willing to trust his own judgement. Asch found that conformity rose when people had to make judgements that were more difficult.

AO3 question: Briefly evaluate learning theory as an explanation of attachment. (4 marks)

Answer Learning theory is the behaviourist explanation of attachment, based on classical and operant conditioning. Harlow's study with monkeys showed that this explanation was wrong. In this study baby monkeys had a choice of a wire mother with a feeding bottle or one covered in cloth. They choose the one covered in cloth. This shows that attachment is not related to feeding as the behaviourists predicted.

Another criticism of the learning theory of attachment is that it is only focused on behaviour and does not include other factors that may influence attachment, such as interactional synchrony.

Examiner comments

Level	Marks	Knowledge	Accuracy	Clarity and organisation	Specialist terminology
2	3–4	Evident	Mostly accurate	Mostly clear and coherent	Effective use
1	1–2	Limited	Lacks accuracy	Lacks clarity, poorly organised	Absent or inappropriately used
	0	No relevant content			

Comments The first two sentences contribute nothing and the final sentence is on findings. That leaves some fairly limited description about the methods. The answer is mostly accurate but lacks clarity because of the irrelevant material. There is a lack of specialist terminology. Level 1, tempted by band above. 2 marks.

Level	Marks	Knowledge	Application	Clarity and organisation
3	5–6	Clear and generally well-detailed	Mostly clear and effective	Coherent and effective use of specialist terminology
2	3–4	Evident	Some effective	Appropriate, lacks clarity in places
1	1–2	Limited	Absent or inappropriate	Specialist terminology absent or inappropriate
	0	No relevant content		

Comments A thorough answer where the student has focused very clearly on the stem at the beginning of each paragraph and linked this to Asch's research.

With reference to the mark scheme we can see that the level of knowledge is clear and reasonably well-detailed – more so in the first paragraph. In the other paragraphs some finer details of the research are missing.

The application is mostly clear and effective. The student has gone beyond simply mentioning 'Sam' in that there are references to the new nightclub and the band he likes.

The answer is coherent but not effective in use of terminology.

Level 3 response, tempted by band below. 5 marks.

Level	Marks	Evaluation	Explanation	Focus	Coherence and organisation	Specialist terminology
2	3–4	Relevant and not generic	Well-explained	Focused	Mostly coherent and organised	Effective use
1	1–2	Relevant	Limited explanation	Limited focus	Lacks clarity, poorly organised	Absent or inappropriately used
	0	No relevant content				

Comments The first sentence is irrelevant. Harlow's study is an appropriate criticism. The description of findings is necessary to draw the conclusion. A reasonably explained point – between Level 1 and 2.

The second criticism is briefer and lacks clarity. This pulls the mark into a Level 1 response. 2 marks.

Understanding marking

AO1 + AO3 question: **Outline and evaluate the behavioural approach to treating phobias.** *(12 marks)*

Answer Phobias are a class of mental disorder associated with high levels of anxiety and avoidance of the phobic object. The behavioural approach to treating phobias is based on explaining phobias using the behavioural approach. Classical conditioning can be used to explain how they are acquired and the same thing can be used in their treatment. The method is called systematic desensitisation. This is based on the principles of conditioning, which is a behaviourist idea.

The steps involved are (1) Patient taught to relax, (2) Create a hierarchy, (3) Start with least feared object and relax, (4) Work way to most feared. This can be done through flooding instead where the hierarchy is missed out and you just go start to the most feared object. This has the difficulty of being quite traumatic and then the patient may just give up, meaning that the therapy is not successful at all.

This has proved to be a good therapy and it makes sense because if people learn a phobia because of conditioning then it can be unlearned. Many patients like this kind of therapy because you don't have to think about it. It's also good because you don't actually need a therapist to do it. If you read about it you could use it yourself to overcome a phobia.

On the negative side, as I have already said, some patients may find it quite unpleasant and if they give up this means it won't be a very useful therapy. Behaviourist ideas are based on research with animals. In fact systematic desensitisation comes from experiments that were first done with cats, so the question is whether it really can be applied to humans. But often this is not true. An alternative might be to use drug therapies or CBT, both of which are effective ways to treat some mental disorders.

A real problem for systematic desensitisation is that it may just cure the symptoms. It could be that there was some deeper psychological cause of the disorder and this is not tackled using systematic desensitisation. All that is cured is the fear of an object rather than actual cause.

356 words

Examiner comments

Introduction contains little of merit, basic scene setting in mentioning classical conditioning and identifying systematic desensitisation.

Very brief outline of an anxiety hierarchy which could be more clearly linked to phobias by using examples. Thus this is lacking detail.

The paragraph also contains a mention of flooding with a criticism.

A number of positive points strung together, only partly effective because there is not much explanation.

Seeing how questions are marked helps you see how to improve your own answers.

Repeat of previous point.

Second sentence onwards is a reasonably developed point, i.e. mostly effective.

Final paragraph is also mostly effective as the point is explained / elaborated.

Level	AS level	Knowledge	Accuracy	Evaluation	Focus	Clarity and organisation	Specialist terminology
4	10–12	Generally well-detailed	Accurate	Effective	Focused	Clear and coherent	Used effectively. Minor detail and/or expansion is sometimes lacking
3	7–9	Evident	Occasional inaccuracies	Mostly effective	Lacks focus in places	Mostly clear and organised	Mostly used appropriately
2	4–6	Present	Lacks accuracy	Partly effective	Mainly descriptive	Lacks clarity and organisation in places	Used inappropriately on occasions
1	1–3	Limited	Many inaccuracies	Limited or absent	Poorly focused	Lacks clarity, poorly organised	Absent or inappropriately used
0		No relevant content					

Overall comments

Knowledge: present, not detailed.

Accuracy: reasonable.

Evaluation: two points that are mostly effective and a number that are partly effective. Ratio of AO3 to AO1 is good.

Focus: lacks focus at the start.

Clarity and organisation: mostly clear but towards lower end of level.

Specialist terminology: mostly used appropriately but towards lower end of level.

Overall the level that best describes this answer is Level 3 but we are tempted lower, making this 7 marks, probably Grade D.

Conformity: Types and explanations

Spec spotlight

Types of conformity: internalisation, identification and compliance.

Explanations for conformity: informational social influence and normative social influence.

Have you heard? Conformity is all about following the others.

REVISION BOOSTER

Feel free to use examples as part of your AO1 description. It's an excellent way to demonstrate your knowledge and understanding of key concepts in conformity, such as internalisation, identification and compliance.

Two-process theory

Deutsch and Gerard (1955) brought ISI and NSI together in their two-process theory of social influence.

They argued that people conform because of two basic human needs: the need to be right (ISI) and the need to be liked (NSI).

Types of conformity

Internalisation	When a person genuinely accepts group norms. It results in a private as well as public change of opinions/behaviour.
	The change is more likely to be permanent and persist in the absence of group members because attitudes have become part of how the person thinks (internalised).
Identification	When we identify with a group that we value, we want to become part of it.
	So we publically change our opinions/behaviour, even if we don't privately agree with everything the group stands for.
Compliance	Involves 'going along with others' in public, but privately not changing opinions/behaviour.
	This results in only a superficial change and the opinion/behaviour stops as soon as group pressure ceases.

Explanations for conformity

Informational social influence (ISI)

ISI is about information, a desire to be right.	Often we are uncertain about what behaviour or beliefs are right or wrong. You may not know the answer to a question in class, but if most of other students agree, you go along with them because you feel they are probably right.
	ISI is a **cognitive** process – people generally want to be right.
ISI occurs in situations that are ambiguous.	ISI is most likely in situations which are new or where there is some ambiguity, so it isn't clear what is right.
	It may happen when decisions have to be made quickly, and when one person or group is regarded as being more expert.

Normative social influence (NSI)

NSI is about norms, a desire to behave like others and not look foolish.	NSI concerns what is 'normal' or typical behaviour for a social group (i.e. norms). Norms regulate the behaviour of groups and individuals so it is not surprising that we pay attention to them.
	NSI is an emotional rather than cognitive process – people prefer social approval rather than rejection.
NSI occurs in unfamiliar situations and with people you know.	NSI is most likely in situations where you don't know the norms and look to others about how to behave.
	It is important with people you know rather than strangers because people are concerned about the social approval of friends.
	It may be more pronounced in stressful situations where people have a need for social support.

A strength of ISI is that there is research support.

Lucas *et al.* (2006) asked students to give answers to easy and more difficult maths problems.

There was more conformity to incorrect answers when the problems were difficult. This was most true for students who rated their maths ability as poor.

People conform in situations where they feel they don't know the answer (ISI). We look to others and assume they know better than us and must be right.

A limitation of ISI is that there are individual differences.

Asch (1955) found that students were less conformist (28%) than other participants (37%).

Perrin and Spencer's (1980) also found less conformity in students – in this study they were engineering students (i.e. confident about precision).

People who are knowledgeable and/or more confident are less influenced by the apparently 'right' view of a majority. Therefore there are differences in how individuals respond to ISI.

A limitation of ISI and NSI is that the 'two-process' approach is oversimplified.

This approach states that behaviour is due to either NSI or ISI.

However, conformity was reduced when there was a dissenting partner in the Asch experiment. This dissenter may reduce the power of NSI (by providing social support) or reduce the power of ISI (because they are an alternative source of information).

Therefore it isn't always possible to know whether NSI or ISI is at work. This questions the view of ISI and NSI as operating independently in conforming behaviour.

A strength of NSI is that there is research support.

Asch (1951) asked participants to explain why they agreed with the wrong answer. Some said they felt self-conscious giving the right answer and were afraid of disapproval.

When Asch asked participants to write down their answers, conformity rates fell to 12.5%.

This supports the participants' own reports that they were conforming because of NSI.

A limitation of NSI is that there are individual differences.

People who care more about being liked are more affected by NSI. They are *nAffiliators* – people who have a greater need for social relationships.

McGhee and Teevan (1967) found that students who were nAffiliators were more likely to conform.

The desire to be liked underlies conformity for some people more than others. One general theory does not cover the fact there are differences.

Apply it

A man is lying on the pavement in a busy street. People are walking round him and ignoring him. No-one stops to see if there is anything wrong.

Miriam hated reading Fifty Shades of Grey for her book group, but at the meeting said she loved it along with everyone else.

Which of these scenarios shows ISI and which NSI? Give some reasons for your choice. Can you think of any more examples?

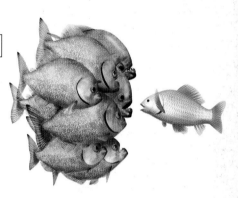

Sometimes it's tough swimming against the tide.

KNOWLEDGE CHECK

1. Give brief explanations of the terms 'internalisation', 'identification' and 'compliance'.
   (2 marks + 2 marks + 2 marks)

2. Outline informational social influence and normative social influence.
   (3 marks + 3 marks)

3. Evaluate informational social influence and normative social influence as explanations of conformity.
   (6 marks)

4. Outline and evaluate research into explanations of conformity.
   (12 marks AS, 16 marks AL)

Conformity: Asch's research

Spec spotlight

Variables affecting conformity including group size, unanimity and task difficulty as investigated by Asch.

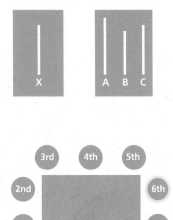

Participants saw two large cards (top). On one was a 'standard line'. On the second card were three other lines. One of the three lines was the same length as the standard and the other two were always clearly different. The participant stated which of the three lines matched the standard.

Each naïve participant sat last or next to last and was not aware that the others in the group were confederates.

Apply it

Some friends are planning what they might do at the weekend. Most of them want to try out a new nightclub. But Sam fancies going to see a band he likes instead.

Briefly explain how each of the factors of group size, unanimity and task difficulty might influence whether or not Sam conforms to the majority.

Key study 1: Asch (1951) Conformity research

PROCEDURE

Solomon Asch recruited 123 American male students. Each was tested individually with a group of between six and eight **confederates** (see diagram, left).

On each trial participants identified the length of a standard line.

On the first few trials confederates gave correct answers but then all selected the same wrong answers. Each participant completed 18 trials. On 12 'critical trials' confederates gave the wrong answer.

FINDINGS AND CONCLUSIONS

The naïve participants gave a wrong answer 36.8% of the time (i.e. the proportion of critical trials when the participants agreed with the confederates' wrong answers).

This shows a high level of conformity, called the *Asch effect* – the extent to which people conform even in an unambiguous situation.

There were considerable individual differences: 25% of the participants never gave a wrong answer, so 75% conformed at least once. A few participants conformed most of the time.

Most participants said they conformed to avoid rejection (*normative social influence*) and continued to privately trust their own opinions (*compliance*, going along with others publicly, but not privately).

Key study 2: Asch (1955) Variables affecting conformity

PROCEDURE

Group size: The number of confederates varied between 1 and 15.

Unanimity: Asch introduced a truthful confederate or a confederate who was dissenting but inaccurate.

Task difficulty: Asch made the line-judging task harder by making the stimulus line and the comparison lines more similar in length.

FINDINGS AND CONCLUSIONS

Group size: With two confederates, conformity to the wrong answer was 13.6%; with three it rose to 31.8%. Adding any more confederates made little difference.

Unanimity: The presence of a dissenting confederate reduced conformity, whether the dissenter was giving the right or wrong answer. The figure was, on average, 25% wrong answers. Having a dissenter enabled a naïve participant to behave more independently.

Task difficulty: Conformity increased when the task was more difficult. So *informational social influence* plays a greater role when the task becomes harder. The situation is more ambiguous, so we are more likely to look to others for guidance and assume they are right.

One limitation is that Asch's findings may be a 'child of the times'.

Perrin and Spencer (1980) found just one conforming response in 396 trials. Participants (UK engineering students) felt more confident measuring lines than Asch's original sample, so were less conformist.

Also, the 1950s were a conformist time in America and people might be less likely to conform in subsequent decades.

The Asch effect is not consistent over time, so is not an enduring feature of human behaviour.

A second limitation is that the situation and task were artificial.

Participants knew they were in a study so may have just responded to **demand characteristics**.

The line task was trivial so there was no reason not to conform. Also, the naïve participants were in a 'group', but not like groups found in everyday life.

Findings do not **generalise** to everyday situations where consequences of conformity are important, and where we interact with groups more directly.

Another limitation is that the findings only apply to certain groups.

Only men were tested by Asch. Neto (1995) suggested that women might be more conformist, possibly because they are more concerned about social relationships (and being accepted).

Participants were from the USA, an **individualist** culture (people are more concerned with themselves than their social group). Smith and Bond (1998) suggest that conformity rates are higher in **collectivist** cultures (e.g. China) which are more concerned with group needs.

This suggests that conformity levels are sometimes even higher than Asch found; his findings may be limited to American men.

Another limitation is that the findings only apply to certain situations.

Participants answered out loud and were with a group of strangers they wanted to impress. Conformity could be higher than usual.

But Williams and Sogon (1984) found conformity was higher when the majority were friends rather than strangers.

Therefore the Asch effect varies depending on circumstances.

There are ethical issues associated with Asch's research.

Naïve participants were deceived. They thought the others in the procedure (confederates) were genuine.

But this ethical cost should be weighed against the benefits of the study.

The main benefit was highlighting people's susceptibility to group conformity and the variables affecting it.

REVISION BOOSTER

When you evaluate Asch's research, don't be sidetracked into describing it first. It can be tempting to do this just to 'set the scene'. There is virtually no description of Asch's procedures or findings on this AO3 page. Follow this example, and stick to evaluation.

And they say social networking is killing the art of conversation.

REVISION BOOSTER

On the left we have identified FIVE evaluation points, and for each provided THREE levels of elaboration.

On page 6 we suggested there are two routes for doing evaluation in an AS essay (6 marks AO3) – either do THREE well-elaborated points or FIVE 'intermediate' evaluations.

KNOWLEDGE CHECK

1. Describe the procedure and findings of Asch's research into conformity. *(6 marks)*
2. Referring to Asch's research, briefly explain how group size, unanimity and task difficulty affect conformity. *(2 marks + 2 marks + 2 marks)*
3. Evaluate Asch's research into conformity. *(6 marks)*
4. Outline and evaluate Asch's research. *(12 marks AS, 16 marks AL)*

Conformity to social roles: Zimbardo's research

Spec spotlight

Conformity to social roles as investigated by Zimbardo.

Life was hard at the Premier Lodge, Prestatyn.

REVISION BOOSTER

There are two major elements to describing Zimbardo's research – what he did (the procedure) and what he found (his results). You can also include conclusions as part of what he found.

Be prepared – you may have to describe just the procedure, or just the findings, or possibly both.

The Lucifer Effect

Zimbardo has in recent years developed his research to try and explain why good people can do evil things. He argues that evil behaviour is not the result of a few 'bad apples' contaminating the rest of the apples in the barrel. Instead, the barrel itself is rotten and it turns the apples in it rotten too. He calls this the Lucifer Effect and claims that it explains the behaviour of the guards in the SPE.

Key study: The Stanford Prison Experiment (SPE)

PROCEDURE

Philip Zimbardo and his colleagues (Haney *et al.* 1973) set up a mock prison in the basement of the psychology department at Stanford University to test whether the brutality of prison guards was the result of sadistic personalities or whether it was created by the situation.

They recruited 24 'emotionally stable' students determined by psychological testing – **randomly assigned** roles of guards or prisoners.

To increase realism, 'prisoners' were arrested in their homes and delivered to the 'prison' – blindfolded, strip-searched, deloused and issued a uniform and number.

The prisoners' daily routines were heavily regulated. There were 16 rules to follow, enforced by guards working in shifts, three at a time.

De-individuation (losing a sense of personal identity):

- Prisoners' names were never used, only their numbers.
- Guards had their own uniform – wooden club, handcuffs, keys and mirror shades. They were told they had complete power over the prisoners, for instance deciding when they could go to the toilet.

FINDINGS AND CONCLUSIONS

Within two days, the prisoners rebelled against their treatment. They ripped their uniforms and shouted and swore at the guards, who retaliated with fire extinguishers.

Guards harassed the prisoners constantly by conducting frequent headcounts, sometimes in the middle of the night.

Guards highlighted the differences in social roles by creating opportunities to enforce the rules and punish slight misdemeanours.

The guards took up their roles with enthusiasm. Their behaviour threatened the prisoners' psychological and physical health. For example:

1. After the rebellion was put down, the prisoners became subdued, anxious and depressed.
2. Three prisoners were released early because they showed signs of psychological disturbance.
3. One prisoner went on hunger strike; the guards attempted to force-feed him and punished him by putting him in 'the hole', a tiny dark closet.

The study was stopped after six days instead of the planned eight days.

The simulation revealed the power of the situation to influence people's behaviour. Guards, prisoners and researchers all conformed to their social roles within the prison.

The more the guards identified with their roles, the more brutal and aggressive their behaviour became.

A strength of the SPE is that the researchers had some control over variables.

Emotionally stable participants were recruited and randomly assigned the roles of guard or prisoner.

The guards and prisoners had those roles only by chance. So their behaviour was due to the pressures of the situation and not their personalities.

Control increases the study's **internal validity**. We can be more confident in drawing conclusions about the influences of social roles on behaviour.

A potential limitation with the SPE is a lack of realism.

Banuazizi and Mohavedi (1975) suggest participants were play-acting. Their performances reflected stereotypes of how prisoners and guards are supposed to behave.

One guard based his role on a character from the film *Cool Hand Luke*. Prisoners rioted because they thought that is what real prisoners did.

But Zimbardo's data showed 90% of the prisoners' conversations were about prison life. The simulation seemed real to them, increasing the study's internal validity.

Fromm (1973) argues that Zimbardo understated dispositional influences.

Only a third of the guards behaved brutally. Another third applied the rules fairly. The rest supported the prisoners, offering them cigarettes and reinstating privileges.

Zimbardo's conclusion – that participants conformed to social roles – may be over-stated, exaggerating the power of the situation.

The differences in the guards' behaviour show that they could exercise right and wrong choices, despite situational pressures to conform to a role.

SPE lacks research support and has been contradicted by subsequent research.

Reicher and Haslam (2006) partially **replicated** the SPE, with different findings. Prisoners eventually took control.

Tajfel's (1981) *social identity theory* (SIT) explains this. Guards in the replication failed to develop shared social identity as a group, but prisoners did and refused to accept limits of their assigned roles.

So the brutality of the guards in the original SPE was due to a shared social identity as a cohesive group, rather than conformity to their social roles.

A limitation is that there were major ethical issues with the SPE.

One issue arose because Zimbardo was both lead researcher and prison superintendent.

A student who wanted to leave the study spoke to Zimbardo, who responded as a superintendent worried about the running of his prison rather than as a researcher.

This limited Zimbardo's ability to protect his participants from harm because his superintendent role conflicted with his lead researcher role.

Apply it

Jane Elliott, a schoolteacher, told the children in her class that people with blue eyes are superior to those with brown eyes because they are more intelligent. She organised her class on this basis, for example she gave privileges to the blue-eyed children only. All of the children started to behave in ways that matched this blue/brown division.

With reference to Zimbardo's research, briefly explain this behaviour in terms of conformity to social roles.

Zimbardo's volunteers knew in advance if they were going to play the part of a prison inmate. Being arrested and strip-searched probably came as more of a surprise…

KNOWLEDGE CHECK

1. Outline the procedure and findings of **one** study into conformity to social roles.
   (6 marks)
2. Briefly describe Zimbardo's research into conformity to social roles. *(4 marks)*
3. Briefly discuss **two** criticisms of Zimbardo's research.
   (6 marks)
4. Outline and evaluate research into conformity to social roles.
   (12 marks AS, 16 marks AL)

Obedience: Milgram's research

Spec spotlight

Obedience as investigated by Milgram.

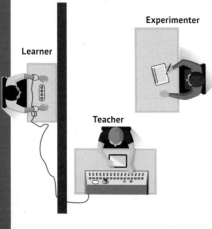

The true participant played the role of teacher, confederates played the other roles. The learner was in a separate room. The setting for this was a lab at Yale University in the US.

REVISION BOOSTER

Milgram is one of a trio of social influence researchers specifically named on the specification (with Asch and Zimbardo). This means you could find yourself writing about the research of any of them. Alternatively, you might need to write about 'social influence' studies, in which case you can choose.

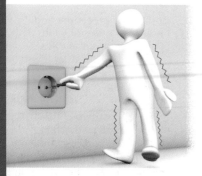

Milgram's research – shocking, in every sense of the word.

Key study: Milgram (1963) Original obedience study

PROCEDURE

Stanley Milgram recruited 40 male participants through newspaper ads and postal flyers. The ad said he was looking for participants for a memory study.

Participants were aged between 20 and 50 years, in jobs ranging from unskilled to professional. They were given $4.50 for just turning up.

Participants drew lots for their role. A **confederate** ('Mr Wallace') was always the 'learner' while the true participant was the 'teacher'. An 'experimenter' (another confederate) wore a lab coat. Participants were told they could leave the study at any time.

The learner was strapped into a chair in another room and wired with electrodes. The teacher had to give the learner an increasingly severe electric 'shock' each time he made a mistake on a task (learning word pairs). The teachers were not told that the shocks were all fake and that Mr Wallace was an actor.

Shocks started at 15 volts (labelled 'slight shock' on the machine) and rose through 30 levels to 450 volts ('danger – severe shock'). At 300 volts ('intense shock') the learner pounded on the wall and gave no response to the next question.

After the 315-volt shock the learner pounded on the wall again but gave no further response.

When the teacher turned to the experimenter for guidance, he gave a standard instruction: 'Absence of response should be treated as a wrong answer'.

If the teacher felt unsure about continuing, the experimenter used a sequence of four standard 'prods':

- (Prod 1) 'Please continue.' or 'Please go on.'
- (Prod 2) 'The experiment requires that you continue.'
- (Prod 3) 'It is absolutely essential that you continue.'
- (Prod 4) 'You have no other choice, you must go on.'

FINDINGS AND CONCLUSIONS

No participant stopped below 300 volts.

Five (12.5%) stopped at 300 volts.

65% continued to 450 volts.

Observations (qualitative data) indicated that participants showed signs of extreme tension; many were seen to 'sweat, tremble, bite their lips, groan and dig their fingernails into their hands'. Three had 'full-blown uncontrollable seizures'.

Prior to the study Milgram asked 14 psychology students to predict the naïve participants' behaviour. They estimated no more than 3% of them would continue to 450 volts. Therefore the findings were unexpected.

Participants were debriefed, and assured that their behaviour was normal. In a follow-up questionnaire, 84% reported that they felt glad to have participated. 74% felt they had learned something of personal importance.

A limitation of Milgram's study is that it lacked internal validity.

Orne and Holland (1968) suggest participants guessed the electric shocks were fake. So Milgram was not testing what he intended to test (i.e. obedience).

However, Sheridan and King's (1972) participants gave real shocks to a puppy; 54% of males and 100% of females delivered what they thought was a fatal shock.

So the obedience in Milgram's study might be genuine, 70% of Milgram's participants believed the shocks were genuine.

A strength of Milgram's research is that it has good external validity.

Milgram argued that the lab-based relationship between experimenter and participant reflected wider real-life authority relationships.

Hofling *et al.* (1966) found that levels of obedience in nurses on a hospital ward to unjustified demands by doctors were very high (21 out of 22 nurses obeyed).

Therefore the processes of obedience in Milgram's study can be **generalised**.

Replications have supported Milgram's research findings.

In a French documentary contestants in a reality TV game show were paid to give (fake) electric shocks – when ordered by the presenter – to other participants (actors).

80% gave the maximum 450 volts to an apparently unconscious man. Their behaviour was like that of Milgram's participants, e.g. many signs of anxiety.

This supports Milgram's original conclusions about obedience to authority and shows that his findings were not just a one-off.

Social identity theory (SIT) is an alternative explanation to Milgram's.

Obedience is about group identification. Milgram's participants identified with the experimenter (the science of the study). When obedience levels fell, the participants identified more with the victim.

Haslam and Reicher (2012) suggest the first three 'prods' are appeals for help with science ('experiment requires you continue'). Only the 4th prod demands obedience. Every time this was used, the participant quit.

The participants did not give shocks due to obedience, but due to their identification with the experimenter as a scientist (as explained by *social identity theory*).

A limitation is there are ethical issues associated with Milgram's research.

Baumrind (1964) criticised Milgram's deceptions. Participants believed the allocation of roles was randomly assigned, but it was fixed.

The most significant deception was that participants believed the electric shocks were real. Baumrind objected because deception is a betrayal of trust that damages the reputation of psychologists and their research.

Deception of participants may also make them less likely to volunteer for future research.

Perry's research

Gina Perry (2013) analysed Milgram's archive of tape recordings. She made several discoveries that undermine the validity of Milgram's findings and conclusions, including:

- The 'experimenter' frequently went 'off-script', for example he would vary the wording of the four prods and use them excessively (26 times with one unfortunate participant).

- Participants often voiced their suspicions about the shocks; Perry concludes that most of Milgram's participants realised that the shocks were faked.

Most people would look up to their boss as an example of an authority figure – though it obviously helps if your boss is thirteen feet tall.

KNOWLEDGE CHECK

1. Briefly describe the procedures of Milgram's obedience study. **(4 marks)**
2. Outline the findings of Milgram's study. **(4 marks)**
3. Briefly discuss **three** criticisms of Milgram's study. **(6 marks)**
4. Outline and evaluate Milgram's research. **(12 marks AS, 16 marks AL)**

Obedience: Situational variables

Spec spotlight

Explanations for obedience: situational variables affecting obedience including proximity, location and uniform, as investigated by Milgram.

Superman discovered that not all uniforms are equally authoritative.

Think of a real-life situation (or more than one) in which proximity, location and uniform play a role in whether or not someone decides to obey an order.

Using evidence from Milgram's research, explain how each of these situational factors influences the decision to obey. Make sure your explanations are closely related to the situation(s).

REVISION BOOSTER

An effective way of evaluating research is to offer counter-arguments. For instance, imagine you have explained how Milgram's variations lack validity because of methodological issues. You can then go on to explain the 'other side of the coin'.

For example, manipulating one situational variable (e.g. proximity) at a time in lab conditions can be artificial, but it also allows us to see the effects of each variable on obedience more clearly.

Explanations for obedience based on situational variables

Proximity

In Milgram's original study, the teacher and learner were in the adjoining rooms. The teacher could hear the learner but not see him.

In the *proximity variation*, teacher and learner were in the same room and the obedience rate dropped from 65% to 40%.

In the *touch proximity variation*, the teacher had to force the learner's hand onto a shock plate. The obedience rate dropped to 30%.

In the *'remote-instruction' proximity variation*, the experimenter left the room and gave instructions by telephone. The obedience rate dropped again to 20.5%. The participants also frequently pretended to give shocks or gave weaker ones when they were ordered to.

Location

The location of the obedience study was a run-down building rather than the prestigious university setting where it was originally conducted (Yale University).

Obedience fell to 47.5%. This indicates that the experimenter had less authority in this setting.

Uniform

In the original baseline study, the experimenter wore a grey lab coat as a symbol of his authority (a kind of uniform).

In one variation the experimenter was called away because of an inconvenient telephone call right at the start of the procedure. The role of the experimenter was taken over by an 'ordinary member of the public' in everyday clothes rather than a lab coat.

The obedience rate dropped to 20%, the lowest of these variations.

This suggests that uniform does act as a strong visual authority symbol and a cue to behave in an obedient manner.

Graph showing all the variations.

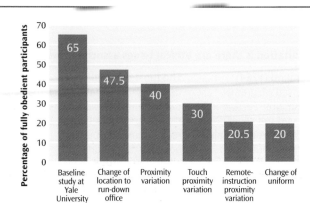

There is research support for the influence of situational variables.

Bickman (1974) looked at the effect of authority on obedience (**confederate** dressed in jacket/ tie, milkman or security guard). The confederate asked passers-by to provide a coin for the parking meter, for example.

People were twice as likely to obey the 'security guard' than the 'jacket/tie' confederate.

This supports Milgram's conclusion that a uniform conveys authority and is a situational factor producing obedience.

A limitation is Milgram's variations may lack internal validity.

Orne and Holland (1968) suggest participants in Milgram's variations were even more likely to realise the procedure was faked because of the extra experimental manipulation.

In the variation where the experimenter was replaced by 'a member of the public', even Milgram recognised this was so contrived that some participants may have worked it out.

So it is unclear whether the results are due to obedience or because the participants saw the deception and 'play acted'.

'Look – if you're going to steal my party outfit idea, the least you can do is lose the hat...'

A strength is that Milgram's research has been replicated in other cultures.

Miranda *et al.* (1981) found over 90% obedience in Spanish students. Milgram's findings are not limited to American males.

However, Smith and Bond (1998) note that most replications have taken place in Western societies (e.g. Spain), culturally not that different from the USA.

It is premature to conclude that Milgram's findings about proximity, location and uniform apply to people everywhere.

A strength is that Milgram's research has control of variables.

Milgram systematically altered one variable at a time to test effects on obedience.

Other variables were kept constant as the study was replicated many times with over 1000 participants.

This control gives us more certainty that changes in obedience were caused by the variable manipulated (e.g. location), showing cause and effect relationships.

A limitation is that Milgram's conclusions provide an 'obedience alibi'.

Milgram's findings are an 'excuse' for obedience – suggesting that it is the situation not the person who is responsible.

Mandel (1998) claims this is offensive to Holocaust survivors to suggest that the Nazis simply obeyed orders and were victims of situational factors beyond their control.

Milgram's situational perspective is dangerous because it ignores the roles that discrimination, racism and prejudice played in the Holocaust.

KNOWLEDGE CHECK

1. Milgram investigated the effects of situational variables on obedience. Briefly outline the findings of his research into any **two** of these variables. *(6 marks)*

2. Evaluate Milgram's research into the effects of situational variables on obedience. *(6 marks)*

3. Outline and evaluate research into the effects of situational variables on obedience. *(12 marks AS, 16 marks AL)*

Obedience: Social-psychological factors

Spec spotlight

Explanations for obedience: agentic state and legitimacy of authority.

Being in an agentic state is like being a 'puppet' of authority – just ask those two.

Apply it

Think about a time when you did something you were told to do (by a parent, teacher, friend, police officer, etc.). Contrast this with an occasion someone told you to do something and you refused.

Explain why you did or did not obey in terms of agentic state and legitimacy of authority.

Eichmann and the Holocaust

Milgram's initial interest in obedience was sparked by the trial of Adolf Eichmann in 1961 for war crimes. Eichmann had been in charge of the Nazi death camps and therefore had a pivotal role in the Holocaust. His defence at his trial was that the important decisions were taken by others in the hierarchy above him and that he was 'only obeying orders'.

Explanation 1: Agentic state

An *agentic state* occurs when we act on behalf of another person.	Milgram proposed that obedience to destructive authority occurs because a person becomes an 'agent', someone who acts for or in place of another. In an agentic state a person feels no personal responsibility for their actions.
The opposite of an agentic state is an *autonomous state*.	'Autonomy' means to be independent or free. So a person in an autonomous state behaves according to their own principles and feels responsible for their own actions.
Agentic shift occurs when a person defers to the authority figure.	The shift from autonomy to being an 'agent' is called the agentic shift. Milgram suggested that this occurs when we perceive someone else as an authority figure. This person has power because of their position in a social hierarchy.
Binding factors reduce the 'moral strain' of obeying immoral orders.	Binding factors are aspects of a situation that allow the person to ignore or minimise the damaging effect of their behaviour and reduce the 'moral strain' they feel. Milgram proposed a number of strategies the individual uses, such as shifting the responsibility to the victim or denying the damage they are doing to victims.

Explanation 2: Legitimacy of authority

We obey people at the top of a social hierarchy.	Most societies are structured hierarchically. People in certain positions hold authority over the rest of us. Parents, teachers, police officers, nightclub bouncers, all have some kind of authority over us at times.
Authorities have legitimacy through society's agreement.	The authority they wield is legitimate in the sense that it is agreed by society. Most of us accept that authority figures should exercise social power over others because this allows society to function smoothly.
We hand control of our behaviour over to authority figures due to trust and through upbringing.	One consequence of legitimate authority is that some people are granted the power to punish others. We give up some of our independence to people we trust to exercise their authority appropriately. We learned to accept authority during childhood from parents and teachers.
Charismatic leaders use their legitimate powers for destructive purposes.	History has too often shown that leaders (e.g. Hitler, Stalin, Pol Pot) use legitimate authority destructively, ordering people to behave in callous, cruel, dangerous and stupid ways.

A strength is that the agentic state explanation has research support.

Blass and Schmidt (2001) showed students a film of Milgram's study and asked them to identify who was responsible for harm to the learner.

Students blamed the 'experimenter' rather than the participant. This responsibility was due to legitimate authority (the 'experimenter' was top of the hierarchy) but also to expert authority (he was a scientist).

The students recognised legitimate authority as the cause of obedience, supporting this explanation.

A limitation is the agentic shift doesn't explain many of the research findings.

Some participants did not obey – humans are social animals in social hierarchies and therefore should all obey.

Also, in Hofling et al's. (1966) study, nurses should have shown anxiety as they gave responsibility over to the doctor, because they understood their role in a destructive process. But this was not the case.

So agentic shift can only account for some situations of obedience.

A limitation is the agentic state cannot account for the behaviour of the Nazis.

Mandel (1998) described German Reserve Police Battalion 101 – men shot civilians in a small town in Poland (World War 2).

They did this even though they were not directly ordered to (they were told they could be assigned other duties).

This challenges the agentic state explanation because the Reserve Police were not powerless to disobey.

Legitimacy of authority is a useful account of cultural differences in obedience.

Countries differ in obedience to authority: only 16% of Australians went to the top of the voltage scale (Kilham and Mann 1974); 85% of German participants did (Mantell 1971).

Authority is more likely to be accepted as legitimate in some cultures. This reflects how different societies are structured and children raised to perceive authority figures.

Supportive findings from cross-cultural research increase the **validity** of the explanation.

A strength is that legitimacy of authority can explain real-life obedience.

Kelman and Hamilton (1989) suggest the My Lai massacre (Vietnam War) is explained by the power hierarchy of the US Army.

The army has authority recognised by the US Government and the law. Soldiers assume orders given by the hierarchy to be legal; even orders to kill, rape and destroy villages.

The legitimacy of authority explanation is able to give reasons why destructive obedience is committed.

'And as a punishment young lady, you can sit on this awful coloured couch for the rest of the day.'

KNOWLEDGE CHECK

1. Outline **one or more** explanations for obedience.
   (6 marks)

2. Describe research into the agentic state explanation for obedience. *(4 marks)*

3. Outline 'legitimacy of authority' as an explanation for obedience. *(4 marks)*

4. Outline and evaluate explanations for obedience. Include the agentic state and legitimacy of authority in your answer.
   (12 marks AS, 16 marks AL)

Obedience: Dispositional explanations

Spec spotlight

Dispositional explanations for obedience: the authoritarian personality.

People with authoritarian personalities get willingly trodden on by those above and are happy to tread on those below.

Dispositional versus situational

Adorno had the same aim as Milgram, to understand the Holocaust. But they came to very different conclusions. Milgram was convinced that everyone has the potential to behave in destructively obedient ways given the 'right' circumstances. This is a situational explanation of obedience. In contrast Adorno believed that the causes of obedience lie within the individual themselves, a dispositional view.

Two students are discussing why some people are more obedient than others. Freda thinks that some people have an 'obedient' type of personality, which developed when they were children. Stefan thinks that we are all capable of being obedient if the situation is right.

What arguments could Freda use to support her view?

Explanation: The authoritarian personality

A high level of obedience is pathological.	Theodore Adorno et al. (1950) wanted to understand the anti-Semitism of the Holocaust. They believed that unquestioning obedience is a psychological disorder, and tried to find its causes in the individual's personality.
Authoritarian personality includes extreme respect for authority and contempt for 'inferiors'.	Adorno et al. concluded that people with an authoritarian personality are especially obedient to authority. They: • Have exaggerated respect for authority and submissiveness to it. • Express contempt for people of inferior social status. • Have conventional attitudes towards race and gender.
Authoritarian personality originates in childhood (e.g. overly strict parenting).	Authoritarian personality forms in childhood through harsh parenting: extremely strict discipline, expectation of absolute loyalty, impossibly high standards, and severe criticism. It is also characterised by conditional love – parents' love depends entirely on how their child behaves.
Hostility towards/fear of parents is displaced onto those who are socially inferior.	These experiences create resentment and hostility in the child, but they cannot express these feelings directly against their parents because they fear reprisals. So the feelings are displaced onto others who are seen as weaker – this is scapegoating. This explains hatred of people seen as socially inferior, a **psychodynamic** explanation.

Key study: Adorno et al. (1950) The authoritarian personality

PROCEDURE	The study investigated unconscious attitudes towards other racial groups of more than 2000 middle-class white Americans.
	Several scales were developed, including the potential for fascism scale (F-scale). Examples from the F-scale: • 'Obedience and respect for authority are the most important virtues for children to learn.' • 'There is hardly anything lower than a person who does not feel great love, gratitude and respect for his parents.'
FINDINGS AND CONCLUSIONS	Authoritarians (who scored high on the F-scale and other measures) identified with 'strong' people and were contemptuous of the 'weak'. They were conscious of their own and others' status, showing excessive respect and deference to those of higher status.
	Authoritarian people also had a **cognitive** style where there was no 'fuzziness' between categories of people, with fixed and distinctive stereotypes about other groups.

There is support for the link between authoritarian personality and obedience.

Elms and Milgram (1966) interviewed fully obedient participants – all scored highly on the F-scale.

However, this link is just a *correlation* between measured variables. We cannot conclude from this that authoritarian personality causes obedience.

A 'third factor' may be involved. Both obedience and authoritarian personality may be caused by a lower level of education (Hyman and Sheatsley 1954).

The authoritarian personality explanation is limited.

Millions of individuals in Germany displayed obedient and anti-Semitic behaviour – but didn't have the same personalty.

It seems unlikely the majority of Germany's population possessed an authoritarian personality.

An alternative explanation is more realistic – *social identity theory* (see page 17). Most Germans identified with the anti-Semitic Nazi state and adopted its views.

A limitation is that the F-scale is politically biased.

Christie and Jahoda (1954) suggest the F-scale aims to measure tendency towards extreme right-wing ideology.

But right-wing and left-wing authoritarianism (e.g. Chinese Maoism) both insist on complete obedience to political authority.

Adorno's theory is not a comprehensive dispositional explanation of obedience to authority because it doesn't explain obedience to left-wing authoritarianism, i.e. it is politically biased.

A limitation is that the explanation is based on a flawed methodology.

Greenstein (1969) suggests the F-scale is 'a comedy of methodological errors', for example items are worded in the same 'direction' so the scale just measures the tendency to agree to everything.

Also, researchers knew the participants' test scores when they interviewed them. So they knew who had authoritarian personalities. They also knew the study's hypothesis, which makes biased results likely.

This suggests that the data collected is meaningless and the concept of authoritarian personality lacks **validity**.

A further limitation is that much of the research uses correlations.

Adorno measured many variables and found significant correlations between them (e.g. authoritarianism correlated with prejudice against minority groups).

No matter how strong a correlation between two variables is, it does not mean that one causes the other.

Therefore Adorno could not claim that harsh parenting style *caused* development of an authoritarian personality.

'I'm only shouting at you for your own benefit', screamed Toby's dad – 'and so you develop an authoritarian personality in later life', he might as well have added...

Spec spotlight

Explanations of resistance to social influence including social support and locus of control.

Resistance: to refuse to accept or be influenced by something – oh yes, Snowy knew all about that.

REVISION BOOSTER

Some exam questions are accompanied by a 'stem', or invented scenario. They give you the chance to demonstrate your knowledge and understanding of psychology by using it to explain something.

So it's really important that you refer to the stem, not just once but throughout your answer. Don't just make passing references – use quotes from the stem, tease out specific content in the stem that you can explain with your knowledge.

Apply it

It's Saturday afternoon and Sid is deep into his revision for an exam on Monday. Three friends call round to persuade him to drop everything for an evening of 'fun and games'. Sid is tempted, but knows his exam is important.

Explain, in terms of Sid's locus of control (internal or external), whether or not he would go along with his friends. Explain how social support could help him to resist his friends' influence.

Explanation 1: Social support

Conformity is reduced by a dissenting peer (social support).	Pressure to conform is reduced if other people are not conforming. Asch's research showed that the dissenter doesn't have to give the 'right' answer. Simply someone else not following the majority frees others to follow their own conscience. The dissenter acts as a 'model'.
The effect is not long lasting.	Asch's research also showed that if this 'non-conforming' peer starts conforming again, so does the naïve participant.
Obedience is reduced by one other dissenting partner (social support).	Pressure to obey can be reduced if another person is seen to disobey. Milgram's research: independent behaviour increased in the disobedient peer condition (from 35% to 90%). The participant may not follow the disobedient peer but the dissenter's disobedience frees the participant to act from their own conscience.

Explanation 2: Locus of control (LOC)

Internals place control with themselves. *Externals* place control outside themselves.	Julian Rotter (1966) described internal versus external LOC. Internals believe things that happen to them are largely controlled by themselves (e.g. doing well or badly in an exam depends on how hard you work). Externals believe things happen outside their control. If they fail an exam they say it was because they had a bad teacher or had bad luck because the questions were hard.
There is a continuum.	People differ in how they explain successes and failures but it isn't simply about being internal or external. There is a continuum: high internal at one end and high external at the other; low internal and low external lie in-between.
Internals show greater resistance to social influence.	People with internal LOC are more likely to resist pressures to conform or obey. (1) If someone takes personal responsibility for their actions and experiences (good or bad) they are more likely to base their decisions on their own beliefs. (2) People with high internal LOC are more self-confident, more achievement-oriented, have higher intelligence and less need for social approval. These personality traits lead to greater resistance.

Research evidence supports the role of dissenting peers in resisting conformity.

Allen and Levine (1971) found independence increased with one dissenter in an Asch-type study.

This occurred even if the dissenter wore thick glasses and said he had problems with vision (he couldn't judge the line lengths).

So resistance is not motivated by following what someone else says but it enables someone to be free of pressure from the group.

Research evidence supports the role of dissenting peers in resisting obedience.

Gamson et al. (1982) found higher levels of rebellion (i.e. independent behaviour) than Milgram did. Gamson's participants were in groups (to produce evidence that an oil company would use to run a smear campaign).

In Gamson's study 29 out of 33 groups of participants (88%) rebelled.

This shows that peer support is linked to greater resistance.

Research evidence supports the link between LOC and resistance to obedience.

Holland (1967) repeated the Milgram study and measured whether participants were internals or externals.

37% of internals did not continue to the highest shock level (they showed independence). Only 23% of externals did not continue.

So internals showed greater resistance. This support increases the **validity** of the LOC explanation and our confidence that it can explain resistance.

A limitation is not all research supports the link between LOC and resistance.

Twenge et al. (2004) analysed data from American locus of control studies over 40 years (1960 to 2002), showing that people have become more independent but also more external.

If resistance was linked to internal LOC we would expect people to have become more internal.

This challenges the link between internal LOC and resistance. However, the results may be due to a changing society where many things are increasingly outside personal control.

A limitation is the role of LOC in resisting social influence may be exaggerated.

Rotter (1982) found LOC is only important in new situations. It has little influence in familiar situations where previous experiences are always more important.

This is often overlooked. It means people who have conformed or obeyed in specific situations in the past are likely to do so again, even if they have a high internal LOC.

This is a limitation because it means that LOC is only helpful in explaining a narrow range of new situations.

REVISION BOOSTER

Quality is always more important than quantity – but many students don't believe this.

Students generally prefer to give a list of lots of different criticisms instead of explaining just one or two criticisms in detail.

It is more difficult to provide one detailed criticism – which is why that gains more credit than a list-like answer.

KNOWLEDGE CHECK

1. Outline how social support can help people to resist social influence. *(4 marks)*

2. Briefly describe the locus of control explanation of resistance to social influence. *(4 marks)*

3. Outline and evaluate **two** explanations of resistance to social influence. *(12 marks AS, 16 marks AL)*

Minority influence

Spec spotlight

Minority influence including reference to consistency, commitment and flexibility.

Although the other gummy bears would tease him because of his tiny paws and oversized head, Barrington knew that if he could just get one of them on side, the rest would surely follow.

Minority influence *refers to how one person or small group influences the beliefs and behaviour of other people. The minority may influence just one person, or a group of people (the majority) – this is different from conformity where the majority does the influencing. (Conformity is sometimes referred to as 'majority influence'.)*

REVISION BOOSTER

At least six concepts related to minority influence are outlined on this page. A really good description will include most of them (range) and in some detail (depth).

Make your answer clearly structured, so that you deal with each concept thoroughly (e.g. internalisation) before going on to the next one (two types of consistency).

Minority influence

A minority changes the opinions of others through *internalisation*.	Minority influence leads to internalisation – both public behaviour and private beliefs are changed. Three processes: consistency, commitment, flexibility.
Consistency Means the minority's view gains more interest.	Consistency makes others rethink their own views ('Maybe they've got a point if they all think this way and they have kept saying it'). • *Synchronic consistency* (people in the minority are all saying the same thing). • *Diachronic consistency* (they've been saying the same thing for some time).
Commitment Helps gain attention. (e.g. through extreme activities).	Activities must create some risk to the minority to demonstrate commitment to the cause. *Augmentation principle*: majority pay even more attention ('Wow, he must really believe in what he's saying, so perhaps I ought to consider his view').
Flexibility The minority should balance consistency and flexibility so they don't appear rigid.	Nemeth (1986) argued that being consistent and repeating the same arguments and behaviours is seen as rigid and off-putting to the majority. Instead, the minority should adapt their point of view and accept reasonable counter-arguments.
Snowball effect The minority becomes the majority.	Over time, more people become 'converted' – switch from the minority to the majority. The more this happens, the faster the rate of conversion. Gradually the minority view becomes the majority and social change has occurred.

Key study: Moscovici *et al.* (1969) The blue-green slides

PROCEDURE	A group of six people viewed a set of 36 blue-green coloured slides varying in intensity, then stated whether the slides were blue or green.
	The study had three conditions: 1. **Confederates** consistently said the slides were green. 2. Confederates were inconsistent about the colour of the slides. 3. **A control group** – no confederates.
FINDINGS AND CONCLUSIONS	Consistent minority condition: participants gave the same wrong answer on 8.42% of trials; 32% gave the same answer on at least one trial.
	Inconsistent minority condition: agreement fell to 1.25%.
	Control group: participants wrongly identified colour 0.25% of the time.

Research evidence demonstrates the importance of consistency.

Serge Moscovici et al. (1969) found a consistent minority opinion had a greater effect on other people than an inconsistent opinion.

Wood et al. (1994) conducted a **meta-analysis** of almost 100 similar studies and found that minorities seen as being consistent were most influential.

This confirms that consistency is a major factor in minority influence.

Research evidence shows change to minority position involves deeper thought.

Martin et al. (2003) gave participants a message supporting a particular viewpoint, and attitudes measured. Then they heard an endorsement of the view from either a minority or a majority. Finally they heard a conflicting view; attitudes measured again.

People were less willing to change their opinions to the new conflicting view if they had listened to a minority group than if they listened to a majority group.

This suggests that the minority message had been more deeply processed and had a more enduring effect.

A limitation is minority influence research often involves artificial tasks.

Moscovici's task was identifying the colour of a slide, far removed from how minorities try to change majority opinion in real life.

In jury decision-making and political campaigning, outcomes are vastly more important, maybe a matter of life or death.

Findings of studies lack **external validity** and are limited in what they tell us about how minority influence works in real-life situations.

Research supports the involvement of internalisation in minority influence.

Moscovici varied his study: participants wrote their answers down, so their responses were private. Agreement with the minority was greater.

This shows that internalisation took place. Members of the majority had been reluctant to admit their 'conversion' publically.

This shows people may be influenced by a minority but don't admit it, therefore the effect of the minority is not apparent.

Applications of minority influence research are limited.

Studies make a clear distinction between majority and minority, but real-life situations are more complicated.

The difference is about more than just numbers. Majorities usually have power and status. Minorities are committed and tight-knit groups whose members know and support each other.

Minority influence research rarely reflects the dynamics of these groups so findings may not apply to real-life minority influence situations which exert a more powerful influence.

Critics have suggested that getting people to persuade others that blue is green is not really something that would happen in everyday life. Having said that, I'm sure we've all met someone who would argue black is white, just for the sheer hell of it.

Apply it

A campaigner against obesity argues that the main culprit is sugar. His solution is to cut out from our diet all cakes, biscuits, sweets, chocolate and fizzy drinks. Not surprisingly, as most people enjoy these foods, they are not keen to accept the message.

Explain **three** ways in which the campaigner might be able to persuade the majority to change their view.

KNOWLEDGE CHECK

1. Explain what is meant by 'minority influence'. *(2 marks)*
2. Outline the procedures and findings of **one** study into minority influence. *(6 marks)*
3. Explain the importance of consistency, commitment and flexibility in minority influence. *(6 marks)*
4. Outline and evaluate research into minority influence. *(12 marks AS, 16 marks AL*

Social influence and social change

Spec spotlight

The role of social influence processes in social change.

The snowball effect – a great thing when it leads to positive social change. When it leads to an avalanche – not so good.

Apply it

A psychology teacher is explaining to her students how times have changed: 'When I was your age, 30 years ago, homosexuality was viewed by most people as wrong and sinful. Not long before that, it was even officially considered by psychology and psychiatry to be a mental illness. Nowadays, the majority of people in Britain are much more accepting and are even in favour of gay marriage.'

Referring to the teacher's comment, explain how social influence processes can lead to social change.

Examples of social change
The example of social change used here is the movement for African-American civil rights in the 1960s. But there are many other cases of change where social influence has been crucial, such as: the spread of environmentalism (e.g. recycling), the eradication of apartheid in South Africa, the collapse of Communism in Eastern Europe, the campaign for women's votes (the Suffragette movement), the growth of the Internet....

Lessons from minority influence research

(1) Civil rights marches drew attention to segregation.	Segregation in 1950s America: places such as schools and restaurants in the Southern States were exclusive to whites. Civil rights marches drew attention to the situation by providing social proof of the problem.
(2) A minority marched but they were consistent.	People took part in the marches on a large scale. Even though it was a minority of the American population, they displayed consistency of message and intent.
(3) Deeper processing.	This attention meant that many people who had accepted the status quo began thinking about the unjustness of it.
(4) Augmentation principle.	'Freedom riders' were mixed racial groups who got on buses in the South to challenge separate seating for black people. Many were beaten and suffered mob violence.
(5) Snowball effect.	Civil rights activists (e.g. Martin Luther King) gradually got the attention of the US government. In 1964 the Civil Rights Act was passed, prohibiting discrimination – a change from minority to majority support for civil rights.
(6) *Social cryptomnesia* occurred.	This refers to people having a memory that a change happened but not remembering how. Social change came about but some people have no memory of the events leading to that change.

Lessons from conformity research

Dissenters make social change more likely.	Asch's research: variation where one **confederate** always gave correct answers. This broke the power of the majority encouraging others to dissent. This demonstrates potential for social change.
Majority influence and normative social influence (NSI).	Environmental and health campaigns exploit conformity by appealing to NSI. They provide information about what others are doing, e.g. reducing litter by printing normative messages on bins ('Bin it – others do'). Social change is encouraged by drawing attention to the majority's behaviour.

Lessons from obedience research

Disobedient models make change more likely.	Milgram's research: disobedient models in the variation where a confederate refused to give shocks. The rate of obedience in genuine participants plummeted.
Gradual commitment leads to 'drift'.	Zimbardo (2007): once a small instruction is obeyed, it becomes more difficult to resist a bigger one. People 'drift' into a new kind of behaviour.

Research support for role of normative social influence (NSI) in social change.

Nolan et al. (2008) hung messages on front doors of houses. The key message was most residents are trying to reduce energy usage.

Significant decreases in energy use compared to **control group** who saw messages to save energy with no reference to other people's behaviour.

So conformity can lead to social change through the operation of NSI.

Minority influence is only indirectly effective in creating social change.

Nemeth (1986) suggests the effects of minority influence are indirect and delayed. It took decades for attitudes against drink-driving and smoking to shift.

Indirect: the majority is influenced only on matters related to the central issue, and not the issue itself.

Delayed: effects not seen for some time.

Using minority influence to explain social change is limited because it shows that effects are fragile and its role in social influence narrow.

A limitation is the nature of deeper processing has been questioned.

Moscovici suggested that minority influence causes individuals to think deeply – which is a different **cognitive** process from majority influence.

Mackie (1987) disagrees, arguing that *majority influence* creates deeper processing if you do not share their views. We believe that others think in the same ways as us; when we find that a majority believes differently, we are forced to think hard about their arguments.

So a central element of minority influence is challenged and may be incorrect, casting doubt on the **validity** of Moscovici's theory.

Identification is an important variable overlooked in minority influence research.

Bashir et al. (2013) suggest people are less likely to behave in environmentally friendly ways because they wanted to avoid label of being minority 'environmentalists'.

Participants rated environmental activists negatively ('tree huggers'). Minorities wanting social change should avoid behaving in ways that reinforce stereotypes; off-putting to the majority.

This suggests that being able to identify with a minority group is just as important as agreeing with their views in terms of changing behaviour.

A limitation is there are methodological issues in this area of research.

Explanations of social change rely on studies by Moscovici, Asch and Milgram.

These can be evaluated in terms of methodology, mainly over the artificial nature of the tasks and whether the group dynamics reflect real-life.

These criticisms apply to the evaluation of explanations for the link between social influence processes and social change.

Sometimes it just takes one to get the ball rolling...

...and the rest will follow.

KNOWLEDGE CHECK

1. Briefly explain what is meant by 'social change'. *(2 marks)*
2. Outline the role of social influence processes in social change. Refer to **one** real-life example in your answer. *(6 marks)*
3. Evaluate the role of social influence in social change. *(6 marks)*
4. Outline and evaluate research into the role of social influence processes in social change. *(12 marks AS, 16 marks AL)*

Coding, capacity, duration of memory

Spec spotlight

Short-term memory and long-term memory. Features of each store: coding, capacity and duration.

STM = short-term memory

LTM = long-term memory

Long-term memories are those memories that are enduring – the ones that are with you for a long time.

REVISION BOOSTER

When you learn about any study it is useful to distinguish the procedures (P) from the findings/conclusions (F).

Some exam questions ask you to write about what a researcher did (= P).

Some questions ask you to write about what a researcher did and what they found (= P and F).

You may use a study as evaluation, then only the findings/conclusions are creditworthy.

The good thing about having a bad memory is that jokes can be funny more than once...

Study 1: Baddeley (1966) Coding in STM and LTM

PROCEDURE

Acoustically similar words (e.g. cat, cab) or dissimilar (e.g. pit, few). Semantically similar words (e.g. large, big) or dissimilar (e.g. good, hot).

FINDINGS AND CONCLUSIONS

Immediate recall worse with acoustically similar words, STM is acoustic. Recall after 20 minutes worse with semantically similar words, LTM is semantic.

Study 2: Jacobs (1887) Capacity of STM

PROCEDURE

Digit span: Researcher reads four digits and increases until the participant cannot recall the order correctly.

FINDINGS AND CONCLUSIONS

On average, participants could repeat back 9.3 numbers and 7.3 letters in the correct order immediately after they were presented.

Study 3: Miller (1956) Capacity of STM

PROCEDURE

Miller made observations of everyday practice. For example, he noted that things come in sevens: there are 7 notes on the musical scale, 7 days of the week, 7 deadly sins, and so on.

FINDINGS AND CONCLUSIONS

The span of STM is about 7 items (plus or minus 2) but can be improved by chunking – grouping sets of digits/letters into meaningful units.

Study 4: Peterson and Peterson (1959) Duration of STM

PROCEDURE

24 students were given a consonant syllable (e.g. YCG) to remember and a 3-digit number to count backwards for 3, 6, 9, 12, 15 or 18 seconds.

FINDINGS AND CONCLUSIONS

Students recalled (on average) about 80% of the syllables correctly with a 3-second interval. Average recall after 18 seconds fell to about 3%. Suggesting that duration of STM without rehearsal is about 18 to 30 seconds.

Study 5: Bahrick et al. (1975) Duration of LTM

PROCEDURE

Participants were 392 Americans aged between 17 and 74.
1. Recognition test: 50 photos from participants' high school yearbook.
2. Free recall test: Participants listed names of their graduating class.

FINDINGS AND CONCLUSIONS

Participants tested 48 years after graduation were about 70% accurate in photo recognition. Free recall was less accurate.

A limitation of Baddeley's study is that it didn't use meaningful material.

The words used in the study had no personal meaning to the participants.

When processing more meaningful information, people may use semantic coding even for STM tasks.

This means the results of this study have limited application. We should be cautious about **generalising** the findings to different kinds of memory task.

My short-term memory is really bad...and also my short-term memory is really bad.

A limitation of Jacobs' study is that it was conducted a long time ago.

Early research in psychology often lacked adequate control of **extraneous variables**.

For example, some participants may have been distracted while they were being tested so they didn't perform as well as they might.

This would mean that the results may not be valid because there were **confounding variables** that were not controlled.

However, these results have been confirmed in other research, supporting its **validity**.

Apply it

Nadiya was using a pedestrian crossing when a car came speeding past her, almost knocking her down. She managed to get its registration – PF54 VXR – but had nothing to write it down with.

How long does Nadiya have before she forgets the car's registration (duration); does she have enough room in her STM to remember it (capacity); and what form will her memory of it take (coding)?

A limitation of Miller's research is it may have overestimated capacity of STM.

For example, Cowan (2001) reviewed other research.

He concluded that the capacity of STM was only about 4 chunks.

This suggests that the lower end of Miller's estimate (5 items) is more appropriate than 7 items.

A limitation of Peterson and Peterson's study is the artificial stimulus.

Trying to memorise consonant syllables does not reflect most real-life memory activities where what we try to remember is meaningful.

So it could be argued that this study lacked **external validity**.

On the other hand, we do sometimes try to remember fairly meaningless things, such as phone numbers. So the study is not totally irrelevant.

A strength of Bahrick et al.'s study is that it had high external validity.

Real-life meaningful memories (e.g. of people's faces and names) were studied.

When lab studies were done with meaningless pictures to be remembered, recall rates were lower (e.g. Shepard 1967).

The downside of such real-life research is that confounding variables are not controlled, such as the fact that Bahrick's participants may have looked at their yearbook photos and rehearsed their memories over the years.

KNOWLEDGE CHECK

1. Briefly explain what is meant by the terms 'short-term memory' and 'long-term memory'. *(2 marks + 2 marks)*
2. Explain how psychologists have investigated the duration of short-term memory. *(4 marks)*
3. Briefly describe research into the capacity of short-term memory. *(3 marks)*
4. Outline the findings of **one** study into the duration of long-term memory. *(2 marks)*
5. Describe research into coding in short-term and long-term memory. *(6 marks)*
6. Describe and evaluate research into coding, capacity and duration of **either** short-term memory **or** long-term memory. *(12 marks AS, 16 marks AL)*

The multi-store model of memory

Spec spotlight

The multi-store model of memory: sensory register, short-term memory and long-term memory. Features of each store: coding, capacity and duration.

On the right is the multi-store model of memory. Above is a multi-storey car park. They sound a bit similar. That's pretty much all they have in common. So not that helpful really. Sorry.

REVISION BOOSTER

If you have to describe/outline the MSM, there are two aspects you should include:

- The structure of the model.
- The processes involved.

Structure refers basically to the memory stores, sensory register, STM and LTM. Outline these one at a time. And remember that material from the previous spread is relevant, so you can describe the coding, capacity and duration of these stores.

Process refers to what happens to information as it flows through the memory system. Describe this step-by-step from start to finish: how information gets into memory, how it is passed from store to store (role of rehearsal), and how it is recalled (retrieval from LTM).

Theory: Atkinson and Shiffrin (1968) Multi-store model (MSM)

Separate memory stores.	The MSM describes how information flows through the memory system. Memory is made of three stores linked by processing.

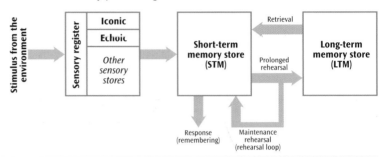

Sensory register (SR).	A stimulus from the environment (e.g. the sound of someone talking) passes into the SR along with lots of other sights, sounds, etc. This part of memory is not one store but five, one for each sense.

- Duration: very brief – less than half a second.
- Capacity: high, e.g. over one hundred million cells in one eye, each storing data.
- Coding: depends on the sense – visual, auditory, etc.

Transfer from SR to STM.	Little of what goes into the SR passes further into the memory system – needs attention to be paid to it.

Short-term memory (STM).	STM is a limited capacity and duration store.

- Duration: about 18 to 30 seconds unless the information is rehearsed.
- Capacity: between 5 and 9 items before some forgetting occurs.
- Coding: acoustic.

Transfer from STM to LTM.	Maintenance rehearsal occurs when we repeat (rehearse) material to ourselves. We can keep information in STM as long as we rehearse it.

If we rehearse it long enough, it passes into LTM.

Long-term memory (LTM).	A permanent memory store.

When we want to recall materials stored in LTM it has to be transferred back to STM by a process called retrieval.

- Duration: potentially up to a lifetime.
- Capacity: potentially unlimited.
- Coding: tends to be in terms of meaning, i.e. semantic.

The MSM is supported by research showing STM and LTM are different.

Baddeley (1966) found that we tend to mix up words that sound similar when using our STMs. But we mix up words that have similar meanings when we use our LTMs.

This clearly shows that coding in STM is acoustic and in LTM it is semantic.

This supports the MSM's view that these two memory stores are separate and independent.

A limitation is that evidence suggests there is more than one type of STM.

Shallice and Warrington (1970) studied KF, a patient with amnesia. His STM for digits was poor when they read them out loud to him. But his recall was much better when he read the digits himself.

The MSM states that there is only one type of STM (unitary store). But KF study suggests there must be one short-term store to process visual information and another to process auditory information.

The working memory model (see next spread) is a better explanation for this finding because it includes separate stores.

Another limitation of the MSM is that it only explains one type of rehearsal.

Craik and Watkins (1973) argued there are two types of rehearsal – maintenance and elaborative. Maintenance is the one described in the MSM.

But elaborative rehearsal is needed for long-term storage. This occurs when you link information to your existing knowledge, or process it.

This is a very serious limitation of the MSM because it is another research finding that cannot be explained by the model.

A limitation is that research studies supporting the MSM use artificial materials.

Researchers often asked participants to recall digits, letters and sometimes words. Peterson and Peterson (1959) even used consonant syllables which have no meaning.

In everyday life we form memories related to all sorts of useful things – people's faces, their names, facts, places, etc.

This suggests the MSM lacks **external validity**. Research findings may reflect how memory works with meaningless material in lab testing, but does not reflect how memory mainly works in everyday life.

A further limitation of the MSM is that it oversimplifies LTM.

There is a lot of research evidence that LTM is not a unitary store.

We have one LTM store for memories of facts about the world (semantic), and a different one for memories of how to ride a bike (episodic).

The MSM is limited because it does not reflect these different types of LTM.

A friend of yours is into acting, and is taking the lead role in Hamlet in a couple of months' time. He needs to learn a lot of lines and be able to remember them long-term.

Using your knowledge of the multi-store model, what advice might you give your friend about how best to remember his lines?

Falling asleep whilst revising – something that would never happen with this book obviously.

KNOWLEDGE CHECK

1. In relation to the multi-store model of memory, explain what is meant by the term 'sensory register'. *(2 marks)*
2. Outline the multi-store model of memory. *(6 marks)*
3. The multi-store model of memory has been heavily criticised. Outline **two** criticisms of this model. *(3 marks + 3 marks)*
4. Describe and evaluate the multi-store model of memory. *(12 marks AS, 16 marks AL)*

Types of long-term memory

Spec spotlight

Types of long-term memory: episodic, semantic, procedural.

'Memories...like the corners of my mind.'
Great song. Except the mind is a metaphysical hypothetical construct and doesn't have corners. Just saying.

Amber is in year five at primary school and has a spelling test every Friday morning. Simon posts on Facebook to describe how he asked his girlfriend to marry him the night before. Finn is in his second karate class where everyone is practising the moves they learned last week.

Identify and explain which types of long-term memory are being used in these situations.

REVISION BOOSTER

You may need to explain a *difference* between two types of LTM (see Knowledge Check). A common mistake when doing this is to describe one type of LTM, then a second type, without a connection between the two. You must identify an actual difference.

A good way of doing this is to choose a feature of memory that one type of LTM has but another type does not. For example, we might say: 'One difference between episodic and semantic memories is the extent to which we are taught them – no one teaches you your episodic memories but many semantic ones are taught.'

LTM store 1: Episodic memory

Stores events (episodes) from our lives.	This store has been likened to a diary of daily happenings. For example, your most recent visit to the dentist, the psychology class you had yesterday, the breakfast you ate this morning.
Episodic memories are complex.	They are time-stamped – you remember when they happened. They involve several elements – people, places, objects and behaviours are woven into one memory. You have to make a conscious effort to recall them.

LTM store 2: Semantic memory

Stores our knowledge of the world.	This is like a combination of an encyclopedia and a dictionary. For example, it includes knowledge of such things as applying to university, the taste of an orange, and the meaning of words.
Semantic memories are not time-stamped.	For example, we do not usually remember when we first learned about 'Justin Bieber'. Semantic knowledge is less personal and more about the knowledge that we all share.

LTM store 3: Procedural memory

Stores memories for actions and skills.	These are memories of how we do things. For example, driving a car or playing table tennis.
Recall occurs without awareness or effort.	These are the sorts of skills we might even find quite hard to explain to someone else because we recall these memories without conscious awareness. For example, explaining how to ride a bicycle or trying to tell someone how you change gear when driving because you do it without having to recall how to do so.

A strength of episodic memory is that it is supported by case study evidence.

Clinical studies of amnesia (HM and Clive Wearing) showed both had difficulty recalling events that had happened to them in their pasts.

But their semantic memories were relatively unaffected (e.g. HM did not recall stroking a dog half an hour earlier, but he did not need the concept of 'dog' explained to him).

This supports the view that there are different memory stores in LTM because one store can be damaged but the others left unaffected.

A strength is that brain scan studies show that there are different LTM stores.

Tulving *et al.* (1994) had participants perform various memory tasks while their brains were scanned with a PET scanner.

Episodic and semantic memories were in the **prefrontal cortex**; semantic in left side and episodic in right prefrontal cortex.

This shows a physical reality in the brain to the different types of LTM, confirmed in many research studies, supporting its **validity**.

A strength is that identifying different LTM stores has real-life applications.

Psychologists can target certain kinds of memory in order to improve people's lives.

Belleville *et al.* (2006) found that episodic memories can be improved in older people with mild **cognitive** impairments. Training led to improvements (compared to **control group**).

This highlights the benefit of distinguishing between different types of LTM – it allows specific treatments to be developed.

A limitation is that there are problems with clinical evidence.

Evidence is often based on clinical cases (e.g. HM and Clive Wearing) about what happens when memory is damaged.

There is a serious lack of control of different variables in these studies (e.g. cannot control the precise location of the brain damage or personality variables).

So it is difficult to **generalise** from these case studies to determine the exact nature of LTM.

A limitation of Tulving's approach is that there may be only two types of LTM.

Cohen and Squire (1980) argued that episodic and semantic memories are stored together in one LTM store called declarative memory (memories that can be consciously recalled).

Cohen and Squire agree that procedural memory is a distinctly different kind of memory to semantic/ episodic, and call it non- declarative.

It is important to get the distinction between semantic and episodic memories right because the way we define them influences how memory studies are conducted.

Ah, the birth of your first child – what a moment that is. It still seems like it was yesterday.

When they handed me this tiny, precious thing – smiling, beautiful, everything in perfect miniature.

I can still remember the feeling of bewildered awe …

… because I'd ordered a pizza.

REVISION BOOSTER

On the left we have identified FIVE evaluation points, and for each provided THREE levels of elaboration.

On page 6 we suggested there are two routes for doing evaluation in an AS essay (6 marks AO3) – either do THREE well-elaborated points or FIVE 'intermediate' evaluations.

KNOWLEDGE CHECK

1. Using an example, explain what is meant by the term 'episodic memory'. *(2 marks)*
2. There are three types of long-term memory. Choose any **two** and explain **one** difference between them. *(2 marks)*
3. Briefly describe **one** type of long-term memory. Use an appropriate example. *(3 marks)*
4. Briefly outline semantic memory as a type of long-term memory. *(3 marks)*
5. Outline and evaluate types of long-term memory. *(12 marks AS, 16 marks AL)*

The working memory model

Spec spotlight

The working memory model: central executive, phonological loop, visuo-spatial sketchpad and episodic buffer. Features of the model: coding and capacity.

You need to know about coding and capacity for each store in the WMM.

CE: coding is flexible; capacity is very limited. (NB Recent views suggest there may be no storage capacity at all.)

PL: coding is acoustic; capacity is about two seconds' worth of what you can say.

VSS: coding is visual and spatial; capacity is three or four objects.

EB: coding is flexible; capacity is about four 'chunks'.

REVISION BOOSTER

The topic of memory can help you to revise more effectively. Consider using mnemonics, a method of improving memory. Try making up a sentence using the letters (in order) of the WMM: CE, PL, VSS, EB. Include one or two rude words because these are especially memorable. Here's a clean attempt: Certain Events Produce Long Very Silly Sausages Every Birthday.

The key phrases in the first column of the table on the right are meant to be triggers to help you remember the main content – see page 7 for an explanation of effective revision.

Theory: Baddeley and Hitch (1974) Working memory model (WMM)

WMM is a model of STM.	An explanation of how STM is organised and how it functions.
	For example, WMM is concerned with the part of the mind that is active when working on an arithmetic problem or playing chess or comprehending language, etc.

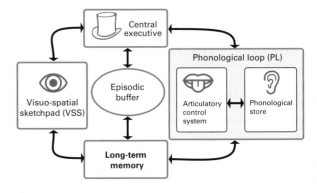

Central executive (CE) allocates slave systems.	Essentially an attentional process which monitors incoming data and allocates slave systems to tasks.
	It has a very limited storage capacity.
Phonological loop (PL) consists of a *phonological store* and an *articulatory process*.	PL deals with auditory information and preserves the order in which the information arrives. It is subdivided into:
	• Phonological store: stores the words you hear.
	• Articulatory process: allows maintenance rehearsal (repeating sounds to keep them in WM while they are needed).
Visuo-spatial sketchpad (VSS).	Stores visual and/or spatial information when required, (e.g. recalling how many windows your house has).
	Logic (1995) subdivided the VSS into:
	• Visual cache: stores visual data.
	• Inner scribe: records arrangement of objects in visual field.
Episodic buffer (EB), temporary storage.	Added in 2000. It is a temporary store for information.
	Integrates visual, spatial, and verbal information from other stores.
	Maintains sense of time sequencing – recording events (episodes) that are happening.
	Links to LTM.

A strength of the WMM is that the case of KF supports separate STM stores.

Shallice and Warrington (1970) carried out a **case study** of patient KF who had brain damage. He had poor STM ability for verbal information but could process visual information normally (difficulty with sounds but could recall letters/digits).

So his phonological loop had been damaged but other areas of memory were intact. This suggests there are separate visual and acoustic stores.

However, evidence from brain-damaged patients may be unreliable because it concerns unique cases of patients who have had traumatic experiences.

Another strength is that dual task performance studies support the VSS.

Baddeley et al. (1975) found participants had more difficulty doing two visual tasks (tracking a light and describing the letter F) than doing a visual and verbal task at the same time.

The greater difficulty is because both visual tasks compete for the same limited resources. When doing a verbal and visual task simultaneously, there is no competition.

Therefore dual task performance activity provides evidence for the existence of the visuo-spatial sketchpad. The MSM can't explain this.

A limitation of the WMM is a lack of clarity over the central executive.

Cognitive psychologists suggest that the CE is unsatisfactory and doesn't really explain anything.

The CE should be more clearly specified than just being simply 'attention'. Some psychologists believe it may consist of separate components.

This means that the WMM hasn't been fully explained.

A strength is that the word length effect supports the phonological loop.

Baddeley et al. (1975) found people have more difficulty remembering a list of long words (e.g. 'association') than short words. This is the word length effect.

This is because there is limited space for rehearsal in the articulatory process (probably about two seconds).

Word length effect disappears if a person is given a repetitive task tying up the articulatory process, demonstrating the process at work.

A further strength of the model is support from brain scanning studies.

Braver et al.'s (1997) participants did tasks involving the CE while they were having a brain scan. Activity seen in an area known as the **prefrontal cortex**.

Activity in this area increased as the task became harder. This makes sense in terms of the WMM: as demands on the CE increase, it has to work harder to fulfil its function.

So this study provides evidence that the CE may have a physical reality in the brain.

Apply it

A car driver is lost so pulls over to ask you for directions. Fortunately, you know where it is they want to get to, so you think for a moment and then describe the route the driver should take.

Explain what is happening in your working memory as you perform this task. Refer to all four components of the working memory store in your explanation.

I don't have an issue with multitasking – I can do several things equally badly at the same time.

KNOWLEDGE CHECK

1. In relation to the working memory model, explain what is meant by the 'phonological loop' and 'episodic buffer'.
(2 marks + 2 marks)

2. Outline the working memory model. *(6 marks)*

3. Outline **two** strengths of the working memory model
(2 marks + 2 marks)

4. Describe and evaluate the working memory model.
(12 marks AS, 16 marks AL)

Explanations for forgetting: Interference

Spec spotlight

Explanations for forgetting: proactive and retroactive interference.

Interference is all about mental confusion between similar tasks – which is why you should never do the ironing when you're expecting a phone call. Ouch!

REVISION BOOSTER

Always remember that there are two major aspects of any research study: what the researchers did (the procedure) and what they found (the findings).

Where do conclusions fit in? You can include these as part of the findings.

Graph showing findings from McGeoch and McDonald's study

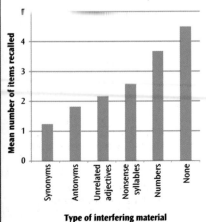

Type of interfering material

Interference theory

Interference: when two pieces of information are in conflict.	Forgetting occurs in LTM because we can't get access to memories even though they are available.
Proactive interference (PI): old interferes with new.	PI occurs when an older memory disrupts a newer one. For example, a teacher learns many names in the past and can't remember names of her current class.
Retroactive interference (RI): new interferes with old.	RI happens when a newer memory disrupts an older one. For example, a teacher learns many new names this year and can't remember the names of her current students.
Interference is worse when memories are similar.	This may be because: • In PI previously stored information makes new information more difficult to store. • In RI new information overwrites previous memories which are similar.

Key study: McGeoch and McDonald (1931) Effects of similarity

PROCEDURE

Participants were asked to learn a list of words to 100% accuracy (i.e. could recall them perfectly).

Then they were given a new list to learn. The new material varied in the degree to which it was similar to the old:
• Group 1: synonyms – words had same meanings as the originals.
• Group 2: antonyms – words had opposite meanings to the originals.
• Group 3: unrelated – words unrelated to the original ones.
• Group 4: nonsense syllables.
• Group 5: three-digit numbers.
• Group 6: no new list – participants just rested (**control condition**).

FINDINGS AND CONCLUSIONS

Performance depended on the nature of the second list. The most similar material (synonyms) produced the worst recall.

When the participants were given very different material, such as three-digit numbers, the mean number of items recalled increased.

This shows that interference is strongest when the memories are similar.

In group 1 it is likely that the words with the same meanings as the original list blocked access or that the new material became confused with the old material.

Evidence from lab studies consistently demonstrates interference in memory.

Many lab experiments have been carried out into interference, (e.g. McGeoch and McDonald's research on the effects of similarity).

Most of these studies show that both types of interference are very likely causes of forgetting from LTM.

Lab experiments control the effects of **extraneous variables** and so give us confidence that interference is a **valid** explanation.

A limitation of the research is the use of artificial materials.

The stimulus material used is often word lists. This is more realistic than consonant syllables, but is still quite different from things we remember in everyday life.

For example, in everyday life we remember people's faces, their birthdays, the ingredients of our favourite pizza, etc.

The use of artificial materials makes interference much more likely in the lab. It may not be a likely cause of 'everyday' forgetting.

A strength is that real-life studies have supported the interference explanation.

Baddeley and Hitch (1977) asked rugby players to recall the names of teams they had played so far in that season, week by week.

Accurate recall did not depend on how long ago the match took place. More important was the number of games played in the meantime.

This study shows that interference explanations can apply to at least some everyday situations.

Another limitation of the research is the time allowed between learning.

Time periods between learning lists of words and recalling them are quite short in lab studies. A participant might learn two lists within 20 minutes.

Research reduces the whole experience of learning into a short time period which does not reflect how we learn and remember most information in real life.

So the conclusions generated from research into forgetting in LTM may not **generalise** outside the lab. The role of interference may be exaggerated.

A limitation is that interference effects may be overcome using cues.

Tulving and Psotka (1971) gave participants five lists of 24 words, each organised into six categories (e.g. metals, fruit, etc.). Categories were not explicit but it was assumed they would be obvious when presented.

Recall was about 70% for the first list, but this fell as each additional list was learned, presumably due to interference. However, when given a cued recall test (told the names of the categories) recall rose again to about 70%.

The memories of the words were stored in LTM but interference prevented access to them. When given a cue, it was easier to access the forgotten words.

Jen's anger at being called by his previous girlfriend's name was not dispelled by John cheerfully pointing out that he had just experienced 'proactive interference'.

KNOWLEDGE CHECK

1. In relation to forgetting, explain what is meant by 'retroactive interference'.
   (2 marks)

2. Briefly explain proactive interference as an explanation for forgetting.
   (2 marks)

3. The interference explanation for forgetting has been criticised. Outline **two** limitations for this explanation. *(2 marks + 2 marks)*

4. Describe **one** study of interference as an explanation for forgetting. In your answer include details of what the researcher(s) did and what they found. *(4 marks)*

5. Discuss interference as an explanation for forgetting.
   (12 marks AS, 16 marks AL)

Explanations for forgetting: Retrieval failure

Spec spotlight

Explanations for forgetting: retrieval failure due to absence of cues.

Every pool player's nightmare – an absence of cues.

REVISION BOOSTER

Retrieval failure theory can help you revise. Meaningful cues can really help you learn and remember because they act as 'triggers'. That's why key terms are useful – to lead you into recall of related material. Headings, subheadings and sub-subheadings (the more the merrier) are also helpful cues, because they mean you organise your material so it is easier to learn and recall.

Even the image below could itself be a cue to the details of Godden and Baddeley's study.

Retrieval failure due to the absence of cues

Lack of cues can cause retrieval failure.	When information is initially placed in memory, associated cues are stored at the same time.
	If these cues are not available at the time of recall, you might not be able to access memories that are actually there.
Encoding specificity principle (ESP).	Tulving (1983) suggested that cues help retrieval if the same cues are present at encoding (i.e. 'coding', when we learn the material) and at retrieval (when we are recalling it).
	The closer the retrieval cue to the original cue, the better the cue works.
Some cues have meaning linked to the memory.	Some cues are linked to the material-to-be-remembered in a meaningful way. For example, the cue 'STM' may lead you to recall all sorts of information about short-term memory.
Some cues have no meaningful link.	Other cues are also encoded at the time of learning but not in a meaningful way: • Context-dependent forgetting: when memory retrieval is dependent on an external/environmental cue (e.g. the weather or a place). • State-dependent forgetting: when memory retrieval is dependent on an internal cue, state of mind (e.g. feeling upset, being drunk).

Key study: Godden and Baddeley (1975) Context-dependent forgetting

PROCEDURE	Cues were the contexts where learning and recall took place – on land or underwater.
	Deep-sea divers learned word lists and were later asked to recall them: • Group 1: Learn on land – recall on land. • Group 2: Learn on land – recall underwater. • Group 3: Learn underwater – recall on land. • Group 4: Learn underwater – recall underwater.
FINDINGS AND CONCLUSIONS	When the environmental contexts of learning and recall did not match (i.e. conditions 2 and 3) accurate recall was 40% lower than when they did match (i.e. conditions 1 and 4).
	When the external cues available at learning were different from the ones at recall, this led to retrieval failure due to lack of cues.
	This study demonstrates context-dependent forgetting because information was not accessible (i.e. was forgotten) when context at recall did not match context at learning.

An impressive range of evidence supports this explanation of forgetting.

For example, Godden and Baddeley's research with deep sea divers.

In fact, Eysenck (2010) goes so far as to argue that retrieval failure is perhaps the main reason for forgetting in LTM.

Supporting evidence increases the **validity** of an explanation, especially when conducted in real-life situations as well as the highly controlled conditions of the lab.

A limitation is that context effects are actually not very strong in real life.

Baddeley (1966) argued that different contexts have to be very different indeed before an effect is seen (e.g. on land versus underwater).

Learning something in one room and recalling it in another is unlikely to result in much forgetting because the environments are not different enough.

So the real-life applications of retrieval failure due to contextual cues don't actually explain much forgetting.

A limitation is context effects only occurs when memory is tested in certain ways.

Godden and Baddeley (1980) **replicated** their underwater experiment using a recognition test instead of recall.

There was no context-dependent effect. Performance was the same in all four conditions whether the environmental contexts for learning and recall matched or not.

This limits retrieval failure as an explanation for forgetting because the presence or absence of cues only affects memory when you test recall rather than recognition.

A limitation is that ESP cannot be tested and leads to circular reasoning.

When a cue produces successful recall of a word, we assume the cue must have been present at the time of learning.

If a cue does not result in successful recall, then we assume that the cue was not encoded at the time of learning.

But there is no way to independently establish whether or not the cue has really been encoded.

A strength is that context-related cues have useful everyday applications.

People often report these experiences: they were upstairs and went downstairs to get an item but forgot what they came downstairs for. But when they go back upstairs, they remember again!

The application is that when we have trouble remembering something, it is probably worth making the effort to revisit the environment in which you first experienced it.

This is a basic principle of the *cognitive interview*, a method of getting eyewitnesses to recall more information about crimes by using a technique called 'context reinstatement'.

Apply it

Doug is a university student who is planning to become a teacher. So he does some work experience at his old primary school, a place he hadn't been anywhere near in almost ten years. But as soon as Doug stepped through the doors, long-forgotten memories of primary school days came flooding back to him.

Explain why this happened to Doug. What does his experience tell us about 'forgetting'?

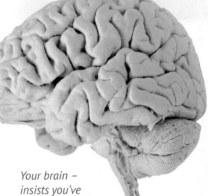

Your brain – insists you've forgotten something, but won't tell you what it is...

KNOWLEDGE CHECK

1. In relation to forgetting, explain what is meant by an 'absence of cues'.   *(2 marks)*
2. Outline retrieval failure as an explanation for forgetting.   *(4 marks)*
3. The retrieval failure explanation for forgetting has been criticised. Outline **two** limitations of this explanation.   *(2 marks + 2 marks)*
4. Describe **one** study of retrieval failure as an explanation for forgetting.   *(4 marks)*
5. Outline and evaluate retrieval failure as an explanation for forgetting.   *(12 marks AS, 16 marks AL)*

Eyewitness testimony: Misleading information

Spec spotlight

Factors affecting the accuracy of eyewitness testimony: misleading information including leading questions and post-event discussion.

A leading question is one that suggests a certain answer because of the way it is phrased. For example, 'Was the knife in his left hand?'. This implies the answer is 'left hand'.

In post-event discussion (PED), witnesses to an event discuss what they have experienced. This could affect the accuracy of their recall.

Apply it

A bank has been robbed by a group of three gunmen in broad daylight. There are at least 15 witnesses to this crime so the police now have a lot of interviewing to do. However, one officer is worried because many of the witnesses know each other and have been discussing the crime. Explain why the police officer is right to be concerned.

Leading questions

Response-bias explanation.	Wording of a question has no enduring effect on an eyewitness's memory of an event, but influences the kind of answer given.
Substitution explanation.	Wording of a question does affect eyewitness memory; it interferes with its original memory, distorting its accuracy.

Key study 1: Loftus and Palmer (1974) Leading questions

PROCEDURE	45 participants (students) watched film clips of car accidents and then answered questions about speed. Critical question: 'About how fast were the cars going when they hit each other?'
	Five groups of participants, each given a different verb in the critical question: hit, contacted, bumped, collided or smashed.
FINDINGS AND CONCLUSIONS	The verb 'contacted' produced a mean estimated speed of 31.8 mph. For the verb 'smashed', the mean was 40.5 mph.
	The *leading question* (verb) biased eyewitness recall of an event. The verb 'smashed' suggested a faster speed of the car than 'contacted'.

Post-event discussion (PED)

Memory contamination.	When co-witnesses discuss a crime, they mix (mis)information from other witnesses with their own memories.
Memory conformity.	Witnesses go along with each other to win social approval or because they believe the other witnesses are right.

Key study 2: Gabbert et al. (2003) Post-event discussion

PROCEDURE	Paired participants watched a video of the same crime, but filmed so each participant could see elements in the event that the other could not.
	Both participants discussed what they had seen on the video before individually completing a test of recall.
FINDINGS AND CONCLUSIONS	71% of the participants mistakenly recalled aspects of the event that they did not see in the video but had picked up in the post-event discussion.
	In a **control group**, where there was no discussion, there were no errors.

A strength is that research into misleading information has real-life applications.

The research has led to important practical uses for police officers and investigators, important because the consequences of inaccurate EWT can be very serious.

Loftus (1975) claimed that leading questions can have such a distorting influence on memory that police officers need to be careful about how they phrase questions when interviewing eyewitnesses.

Research into EWT is one area where psychologists can make an important difference to the lives of real people, e.g. by improving how the legal system works and acting as expert witnesses.

A limitation of Loftus and Palmer's study is that it used artificial materials.

Participants watched film clips of accidents, a very different experience from witnessing a real accident (e.g. it is less stressful).

Yuille and Cutshall (1986) found that witnesses of a traumatic real armed robbery had very accurate recall after four months.

This shows that using artificial tasks tells us little about how leading questions affect EWT in real crimes or accidents.

A limitation is there may be individual differences in accuracy of EWT.

Anastasi and Rhodes (2006) found that older people were less accurate than younger people when giving eyewitness reports.

However, they also found that all age groups were more accurate when identifying people of their own age group (own-age bias).

Research studies often use younger people as the target to identify. So some age groups may seem less accurate but this is not really the case.

Another limitation is that lab studies of EWT suffer from demand characteristics.

Research participants usually want to be helpful and attentive. So when they are asked a question and don't know the answer, they guess, (especially for 'yes/no' questions).

Participants might be asked 'Did you see the blue car?' Even if there was not a blue car in the film, participants may reply 'yes' because it seems a more helpful answer.

This challenges the validity of EWT research. Studies intend to measure the accuracy of eyewitness memory but the answers eyewitnesses give may not actually reflect their memories.

A further limitation is that many EWT research studies lack external validity.

Foster et al. (1994) argue that what you remember as an eyewitness can have important consequences in the real world, but the same is not true in research studies.

Real eyewitnesses search their memory with more effort because their testimony may lead to a successful conviction (or wrongful if inaccurate). This is not true in research studies.

Therefore EWT accuracy may be greater in the real world because of the seriousness with which eyewitnesses undertake their role.

REVISION BOOSTER

Don't confuse evaluation and description. Students often think they are doing well on evaluation and are disappointed to find they haven't got high marks. But this is usually because they aren't evaluating at all – they're just describing. For example, you might evaluate misleading information by pointing to the supporting evidence. But if all you do is say what the evidence is (e.g. what Loftus and Palmer found), that's description.

'So what first attracted you to your millionaire husband?'

An example of a leading question maybe..?

KNOWLEDGE CHECK

1. Explain what is meant by the term 'eyewitness testimony'. (2 marks)

2. In relation to accuracy of eyewitness testimony, explain what is meant by 'misleading information'. (2 marks)

3. Outline two factors that may affect the accuracy of eyewitness testimony. (2 marks + 2 marks)

4. Describe one study into the effects of misleading information on eyewitness testimony. (6 marks)

5. Outline research into post-event discussion as a factor affecting the accuracy of eyewitness testimony. (4 marks)

6. Describe and evaluate misleading information as a factor affecting the accuracy of eyewitness testimony. (12 marks AS, 16 marks AL)

Eyewitness testimony: Anxiety

Spec spotlight

Factors affecting the accuracy of eyewitness testimony: anxiety.

Weapon focus

When a crime involves a weapon, it often attracts the attention of eyewitnesses. The anxiety associated with the weapon may affect recall of the event. This is weapon focus.

REVISION BOOSTER

Yerkes-Dodson can help you with exams: when it comes to performance, a little bit of anxiety is OK. So you shouldn't worry if exams (or even just the thought of them) make you a bit anxious.

But too much anxiety can be crippling, and might prevent you doing some revision or performing at your best on the day. If this applies to you, it's probably a good idea to learn how to reduce anxiety.

One word of advice though – being on top of your revision can be a very good antidote to anxiety.

Yerkes-Dodson Law

This inverted U theory states that performance will increase with stress, but only to a certain point, where it decreases drastically.

Study 1: Johnson and Scott (1976) Anxiety has a negative effect

PROCEDURE

Participants sat in a waiting room believing they were going to take part in a lab study.

Each participant heard an argument in the next room.
- *Low-anxiety condition*: a man then walked through the waiting room carrying a pen with grease on his hands.
- *High-anxiety condition*: the heated argument was accompanied by the sound of breaking glass. A man then walked through the room holding a paper knife covered in blood.

Participants were later asked to pick the man from a set of 50 photographs.

FINDINGS AND CONCLUSIONS

49% of participants in the low-anxiety condition were able to identify him. The corresponding figure for high-anxiety participants was just 33%.

The *tunnel theory of memory* argues that a witness's attention is on the weapon (*weapon focus*), because it is a source of danger and anxiety.

Study 2: Yuille and Cutshall (1986) Anxiety has a positive effect

PROCEDURE

In a real-life crime a gun-shop owner shot a thief dead. There were 21 witnesses, 13 agreed to participate in the study.

Participants were interviewed 4–5 months after the incident. Accounts were compared to the police interviews at the time of the shooting.

Witnesses rated how stressed they felt at the time of the incident.

FINDINGS AND CONCLUSIONS

Witnesses were very accurate and there was little change after 5 months. Some details were less accurate, e.g. colours of items, and age/weight/height.

Participants who reported the highest levels of stress were most accurate (about 88% compared to 75% for the less-stressed group).

Explaining the contradictory findings

'Inverted U' theory.	Yerkes and Dodson (1908) argue that the relationship between performance and arousal/stress is curvilinear rather than linear, as in the diagram on the left.
Affects memory	Deffenbacher (1983) found that lower levels of anxiety did produce lower levels of recall accuracy. Recall accuracy increases with anxiety up to an optimal point. A drastic decline in accuracy is seen when an eyewitness experiences more anxiety than the optimal point.

A limitation of Johnson and Scott's study is that it may test surprise not anxiety.

Participants may focus on a weapon because they are surprised at what they see rather than because they are scared.

Pickel (1998) used scissors, handgun, wallet and raw chicken as hand-held items in a hairdressing salon. EWT accuracy was poorer for high unusualness (chicken and handgun).

So the weapon focus effect is due to unusualness rather than anxiety/threat and therefore tells us nothing specifically about the effects of anxiety on EWT.

A limitation of field studies is that they lack control of variables.

Real-life witnesses are interviewed sometime after the event. Many things happen to them in the meantime that researchers cannot control.

Examples: eyewitnesses discuss the event with others; they read or view accounts in the media; the police interview may influence their memory (*post-event discussions*).

These **extraneous variables** may be responsible for the (in)accuracy of recall, not anxiety. It is difficult to isolate the variables.

Another limitation is that there are ethical issues in this research area.

Creating anxiety in participants is potentially unethical because it may subject people to psychological harm purely for research purposes.

So real-life studies are beneficial: psychologists interview people who have already witnessed an event, so there is no need to create it.

Ethical issues don't challenge the findings of studies (e.g. Johnson and Scott) but they do raise questions about conducting such research.

The inverted-U explanation is limited because it is too simplistic.

Anxiety is difficult to define and measure because it has many elements – **cognitive**, behavioural, emotional and physical.

The inverted-U explanation assumes that one of these is linked to poor performance – physiological (physical) arousal.

The explanation fails to account for other factors; for example the effect of the emotional experience of witnessing a crime (e.g. terror, fear) on the accuracy of memory.

A limitation is that demand characteristics may affect lab studies of anxiety.

Most participants in controlled lab studies are aware they are watching a filmed (and staged) crime for a reason to do with a study.

They may work out that they will be asked questions about what they have seen. They may give responses which they believe to be helpful to the researcher.

So the research is not measuring the accuracy of EWT and this reduces the **validity** of research investigating the effects of anxiety.

Apply it

Shots were fired during an armed robbery, although no-one was hurt. But it was a stressful experience for all the witnesses. A police officer has noticed that, although they both experienced the same event, one of the witnesses seems to have good recall of what happened, but another remembers very little.

Use your knowledge of the relationship between anxiety and recall to explain why the two witnesses might differ in their accuracy.

'You won't get away with this', said the dog. 'Some psychological research suggests that the anxiety created by this situation will enhance my recall of the event.'

'That's as maybe' replied the sheep, 'but you'll never pick me out of a line-up'.

KNOWLEDGE CHECK

1. Describe **one** study into anxiety as a factor affecting the accuracy of eyewitness testimony. Include in your answer what the researcher(s) did and what they found.
   (6 marks)

2. Outline how anxiety may be a factor affecting the accuracy of eyewitness testimony.
   (4 marks)

3. Describe and evaluate anxiety as a factor affecting the accuracy of eyewitness testimony.
   (12 marks AS, 16 marks AL)

Eyewitness testimony: The cognitive interview

Spec spotlight

Improving the accuracy of eyewitness testimony including the use of the cognitive interview.

A witness had described the suspect as being 'a bit on the green side'. It seemed that the police finally had their man.

Apply it

Imagine you are police officer working in a police force that routinely uses the cognitive interview. You are interviewing a witness to a stabbing in which the victim survived but with serious injuries.

For each of the four main techniques of the CI, write the wording of a question you would ask the witness.

*Also, explain **three** ways in which you could use the enhanced CI in this situation.*

The cognitive interview (CI)

Based on psychological understanding of memory.	Fisher and Geiselman (1992) claim that EWT could be improved if the police use techniques based on psychological insights into how memory works.
	They called it the cognitive interview to indicate its foundation in **cognitive** psychology.
	Rapport (understanding) is established with interviewee.
Report everything.	Witnesses are encouraged to include every detail of an event, even if it seems irrelevant or the witness is not confident about it.
	Seemingly trivial details could be important and may trigger other memories.
Reinstate the context.	The witness returns to the original crime scene 'in their mind' and imagines the environment (e.g. the weather, what they could see) and their emotions (e.g. what they felt).
	This is based on the concept of *context-dependent forgetting* (see page 40). Cues from the context may trigger recall.
Reverse the order.	Events are recalled in a different chronological order (e.g. from the end back to the beginning, or from the middle to the beginning).
	This prevents people using their expectations of how the event must have happened rather than the actual events.
	It also prevents dishonesty (harder to produce an untruthful account if it has to be reversed).
Change perspective.	Witnesses recall the incident from other people's perspectives. How would it have appeared to another witness or to the perpetrator?
	This prevents the influence of expectations and *schema* on recall. Schema are packages of information developed through experience. They generate a framework for interpreting incoming information.
Enhanced cognitive interview.	Fisher *et al.* (1987) developed additional elements of the CI.
	This includes a focus on the social dynamics of the interaction (e.g. knowing when to establish and relinquish eye contact).
	The enhanced CI also includes ideas such as reducing the eyewitness's anxiety, minimising distractions, getting the witness to speak slowly and asking open-ended questions.

A strength is that some elements of the full CI are useful.

Milne and Bull (2002) found that each individual element of the CI was equally valuable.

However, they also found that a combination of 'report everything' and 'context reinstatement' produced better recall than any of the other techniques individually.

So at least these two elements should be used to improve police interviewing of eyewitnesses even if the full CI isn't used.

Another strength is the support for effectiveness of the enhanced CI.

A **meta-analysis** by Köhnken et al. (1999) combined data from 50 studies.

The enhanced CI consistently provided more correct information than the standard interview used by police.

Studies like this indicate that there are real practical benefits to the police of using the enhanced version of the CI.

A limitation of the CI is that it is time-consuming.

Police are reluctant to use CI because it takes much more time than the standard police interview. More time is needed to establish rapport with the witness to allow them to relax.

Kebbell and Wagstaff (1997) point out that the CI also requires special training and many forces have not been able to provide more than a few hours.

This means it is unlikely that the 'proper' version of the CI is actually used (which may explain why police have not been that impressed by it).

A limitation is that research may be unreliable because of variations of the CI.

Studies of the effectiveness of the CI inevitably use slightly different techniques.

Different researchers may use variations on the CI or enhanced CI, and police forces evolve their own methods.

This means it is difficult to draw conclusions about the CI in general.

A limitation of the CI is that it produces an increase in inaccurate information.

The techniques of the CI aim to increase the amount of correct information recalled, but the recall of incorrect information may also be increased.

Köhnken et al. (1999) found an 81% increase in correct information but also a 61% increase in incorrect information (false positives) when the enhanced CI was compared to a standard interview.

The increase in correct information implies that police should continue to use CI. However, the results also suggest that police need to treat all information collected with caution.

KNOWLEDGE CHECK

1. Explain what is meant by the term 'cognitive interview'.
   (2 marks)

2. Describe the use of the cognitive interview to improve the accuracy of eyewitness testimony. *(6 marks)*

3. The cognitive interview uses four main techniques to improve the accuracy of eyewitness testimony. Briefly outline any **two** of these techniques. *(4 marks)*

4. Outline **one** method of improving the accuracy of eyewitness testimony. *(4 marks)*

5. Discuss the cognitive interview as a method of improving the accuracy of eyewitness testimony.
   (12 marks AS, 16 marks AL)

'I'm sorry' blurted out the woman desperately as she broke down. 'I just don't think I can learn any more about memory'.

'OK', replied her psychology teacher, 'let's move on to attachment then'.

Caregiver–infant interactions

Spec spotlight

Caregiver–infant interactions in humans: reciprocity and interactional synchrony.

What is attachment?

An attachment is a close two-way emotional bond between two individuals in which each sees the other as essential for their own emotional security. We can recognise an attachment when people display the following behaviours:

- Proximity (staying physically close to the attachment figure).

- Separation distress (being upset when an attachment figure leaves).

- Secure-base behaviour (leaving the attachment figure but regularly returning to them when playing).

Larry is a three-month-old baby. His mother Lucy spends most time with him and is his main caregiver. Larry's father has often noticed how he and Lucy just seem to be 'in tune' with each other when they are playing together.

Using the concepts of reciprocity and interactional synchrony, explain what sort of behaviours you would expect to see from Larry and Lucy.

Reciprocity and interactional synchrony

Newborn babies have alert phases.	From birth, babies and their mothers (or other carers) spend a lot of time in intense and pleasurable interaction.
	Babies have periodic 'alert phases' and signal they are ready for interaction, which mothers respond to around two-thirds of the time (Feldman and Eidleman 2007).
Interactional synchrony = mirroring.	Two people are said to be 'synchronised' when they carry out the same action simultaneously.
	Interactional synchrony can be defined as 'the coordination of micro-level behaviour' (Feldman 2007).
	It takes place when mother and infant interact in such a way that their actions and emotions mirror the other.
Interactional synchrony at two weeks old.	Meltzof and Moore (1977) observed the beginnings of interactional synchrony in infants as young as two weeks old.
	An adult displayed one of three facial expressions or one of three distinctive gestures and the child's response was filmed.
	An association was found between the expression/gesture and the action of the child.
Important for development of attachment. High synchrony = higher quality attachment.	Synchrony provides the necessary foundation for the mother and infant connection which can be built upon in subsequent years.
	Isabella et al. (1989) observed 20 mothers and infants together and assessed the degree of synchrony and the quality of mother–infant attachment.
	The researchers found that high levels of synchrony were associated with better quality mother–infant attachment (e.g. the emotional intensity of the relationship).
Reciprocity – one person responds to the other.	From around three months reciprocal interaction tends to be increasingly frequent, when each person responds to the other and elicits a response from them.
	It involves close attention to each other's verbal signals and facial expressions.
	Brazleton et al. (1975) described this interaction as a 'dance' because it is just like a couple's dance where each partner responds to each other's moves.
Baby is active.	Traditional views of childhood have seen the baby in a passive role, receiving care from an adult. However, it seems that the baby takes an active role. Both mother and child can initiate interactions and they appear to take turns in doing so.

A limitation is that it is hard to know what is happening when observing infants.

Many studies into mother–infant interactions have shown the same patterns of behaviour (Gratier 2003). However, what is being observed is merely hand movements or changes in expression.

It is difficult to be sure, based on these observations, what is taking place from the infant's perspective. For example, is the infant's imitation of adult signals conscious and deliberate?

This means we cannot be certain that behaviours seen in mother–infant interactions have a special meaning.

A strength of the research is that it uses well-controlled procedures.

Mother–infant interactions are usually filmed, often from multiple angles. Very fine details of behaviour can be recorded and analysed later.

Also babies don't know they are being observed, so their behaviour does not change in response to observation (generally the main problem for observation research).

This is a strength of this line of research because it means the studies have good **validity**.

However, observations don't tell us the purpose of synchrony and reciprocity.

Feldman (2012) points out that synchrony (and by implication reciprocity) simply describe behaviours that occur at the same time.

These are robust phenomena in the sense that they can be reliably observed, but this may not be particularly useful as it does not tell us their purpose.

However, there is some evidence that reciprocity and synchrony are helpful in the development of mother–infant attachment, stress responses, empathy, language and moral development.

A limitation is research into mother–infant interactions is socially sensitive.

This is because it suggests that children may be disadvantaged by particular child-rearing practices.

Specifically, mothers who return to work shortly after a child is born restrict the opportunities for achieving interactional synchrony.

This suggests that mothers should not return to work so soon – this has obvious socially sensitive implications.

A strength of this research is its potential value to society.

The identification of interactional synchrony as an important foundation in the formation of high-quality attachments could have practical applications that benefit society.

Crotwell et al. (2013) found that a 10-minute *Parent–Child Interaction Therapy* (PCIT) improved interactional synchrony in 20 low-income mothers and their pre-school infants compared to a **control group**.

The findings suggest that research on interactional synchrony could lead to valuable methods for improving and developing mother–infant attachments (particularly in at-risk groups).

Interactional synchrony has been described as being like a 'dance' between parent and child. 'And it's a ten from Len…'

KNOWLEDGE CHECK

1. In relation to caregiver–infant interactions in humans, explain what is meant by 'reciprocity' and 'interactional synchrony'. *(2 marks + 2 marks)*
2. Outline research into interactional synchrony in humans. *(4 marks)*
3. Outline research into reciprocity in humans. *(4 marks)*
4. Describe and evaluate research into caregiver–infant interactions in humans. *(12 marks AS, 16 marks AL)*

The role of the father

Spec spotlight

The role of the father.

Research suggests that fathers can play an important role in nurturing their child's development. No excuse for the matching outfits though.

REVISION BOOSTER

You will notice that there are six key points for every approach. This would cover what you would need in any essay in terms of descriptive content (both for AS and A level essays because the description is always just 6 marks). Don't be tempted to overdescribe.

Attachment research within this area may be affected by stereotyped assumptions about the roles of mothers and fathers.

Primary attachment usually with mothers but sometimes both.	Schaffer and Emerson (1964) found that the majority of babies became attached to their mother first (this happens around 7 months). In only 3% of cases the father was the first sole object of attachment. In 27% of cases the father was the joint first object of attachment with the mother. Within a few weeks or months they then formed secondary attachments to other family members, including the father.
75% eventually form *secondary attachments* with father.	In 75% of infants studied an attachment was formed with the father by the age of 18 months. This was indicated by the fact the infants protested when their father walked away, a sign of attachment.
Attachment with mother most related to teen attachments.	Grossmann (2002) carried out a **longitudinal** study looking at parents' behaviour and its relationship to the quality of children's attachments into their teens. This research found that quality of attachment with the father was less important in the attachment type of the teenagers than quality of attachment with the mother. Therefore fathers may be less important in long-term emotional development.
Fathers' play is more important.	The quality of fathers' play with infants was related to children's attachments. This suggests that fathers have a different role in attachment, one that is more to do with play and stimulation and less to do with nurturing.
Fathers can be primary caregivers.	Some evidence suggests that when fathers do take on the role of being the main caregiver they adopt behaviours more typical of mothers. Field (1978) filmed 4-month-old babies and found that primary caregiver fathers, like mothers, spent more time smiling, imitating and holding infants than secondary caregiver fathers.
Level of response is most important.	Smiling, imitating and holding infants are behaviours that appear to be important in building an attachment with an infant. So it seems the father can be the more nurturing attachment figure. The key to the attachment relationship is the level of responsiveness not the gender of the parent.

A limitation is researchers are interested in different research questions.

Some psychologists want to understand the role of fathers as secondary attachment figures. But others are more concerned with fathers as a primary attachment figure.

The former have tended to see fathers as behaving differently from mothers and having a distinct role. The latter have found that fathers can take on a 'maternal' role.

This is a limitation because it means psychologists cannot easily answer the simple question: what is the role of the father?

A limitation is the evidence undermines the idea of fathers having distinct roles.

Grossman (2002) found that fathers as secondary attachment figures had an important and distinct role in their children's development, involving play and stimulation.

Other studies (e.g. McCallum and Golombok 2004) found that children growing up in single or same-sex parent families don't develop differently from those in two-parent families.

This suggests that the father's role as a secondary attachment figure is not important.

Research fails to provide a clear answer about fathers and primary attachments.

The answer could be related to traditional gender roles, in which women are expected to be more caring and nurturing than men.

Therefore, fathers simply don't feel they should act in a nurturing way.

Or it could be that female hormones (e.g. oestrogen) create higher levels of nurturing and therefore women are biologically predisposed to be primary attachment figures.

A further limitation is that social biases prevent objective observation.

Preconceptions about how fathers behave are created by common discussions about mothers' and fathers' parenting behaviour.

These stereotypes (e.g. fathers are more playful, stricter, etc.) may cause unintentional observer bias whereby observers 'see' what they expect rather than recording actual reality.

As such, conclusions on the role of the father in attachment are hard to disentangle from social biases about their role.

This research has important economic implications.

Mothers feel pressured to stay at home because of research that says mothers are vital for healthy emotional development.

In some families this may not be economically the best solution – for them or our society in general.

This research may be of comfort to mothers who feel they have to make hard choices about not returning to work.

Apply it

Larry is now eight months old. His dad is much more involved with his son, playing with him regularly every day. But recently he's noticed that Larry tends to go to his mummy for comfort when he is distressed, so he sometimes feels a bit left out and worries that he's not being a 'proper' dad.

Using psychological research, explain why Larry's dad has no need to worry.

REVISION BOOSTER

On the left we have identified FIVE evaluation points, and for each provided THREE levels of elaboration.

On page 6 we suggested there are two routes for doing evaluation in an AS essay (6 marks AO3) – either do THREE well-elaborated points or FIVE 'intermediate' evaluations.

KNOWLEDGE CHECK

1. Briefly explain the role of the father in relation to attachment. *(3 marks)*
2. Outline research relating to the role of the father in attachment. *(6 marks)*
3. Describe and evaluate research into the role of the father in attachment.
   (12 marks AS, 16 marks AL)

Schaffer's stages of attachment

Spec spotlight

Stages of attachment as identified by Schaffer.

Multiple attachments.

6-week-old Nathan still hadn't worked out who his mum was – the large thing talking softly in his ear or the little yellow thing floating in the water.

A child psychologist observes Larry's behaviour at several points throughout his first year, and makes the following notes:

- *Larry becomes very upset when he sees a stranger and can only be comforted by his mum.*

- *Larry grasps every object presented to him, from mummy's finger to his teddy bear. He makes the same gurgling noises at everyone he sees.*

- *Larry seems to recognise other family members (such as his grandparents) and is happy to play with them all.*

- *When Larry cries, he is happy to be comforted by family friends and even babysitters as well as his mum and dad.*

Identify which stages of Larry's development are being described.

Explain your choices and give Larry's approximate age at each stage.

Stages of attachment

Asocial stage (first few weeks).	Baby's behaviour towards inanimate objects and humans is quite similar. Some preference for familiar adults (more easily calmed by them). Babies are also happier in the presence of other humans.
Indiscriminate attachment (2–7 months).	Babies now display more observable social behaviour, with a preference for people rather than inanimate objects. They recognise and prefer familiar adults. Babies do not show *stranger* or *separation anxiety*. Attachment is indiscriminate because it's the same towards all.
Specific attachment (from around 7 months).	Stranger anxiety and separation anxiety when separated from one particular adult. Baby is said to have formed a specific attachment with the *primary attachment figure*. This is in most cases the person who offers the most interaction and responds to the baby's 'signals' with the most skill (the biological mother in 65% of cases).
Multiple attachments (by one year).	*Secondary attachments* with other adults form shortly after. In Schaffer and Emerson's study, 29% of babies had secondary (multiple) attachments within a month of forming a primary (specific) attachment. By the age of one year the majority of infants had multiple secondary attachments.

Key study: Schaffer and Emerson (1964) Stages of attachment

PROCEDURE	60 babies from Glasgow, most from working-class families. Babies and their mothers were visited at home every month for a year and at 18 months. *(longitudinal study).*
	Separation anxiety measured by asking mothers about their children's behaviour during everyday separations (e.g. adult leaving the room). *Stranger anxiety* was measured by asking mothers questions about their children's anxiety response to unfamiliar adults. *AO3 · X SELF REPORT, socially desirable.*
FINDINGS AND CONCLUSIONS	50% of babies showed *separation anxiety* towards a particular adult between 25 and 32 weeks of age. This *specific (primary) attachment* was usually with the mother. *By 40 weeks · 80% specific + 30% multiple formed.*
	Attachment tended to be to the caregiver who was most interactive and sensitive to infant signals and facial expressions (i.e. *reciprocity*). This was not necessarily the person the infant spent most time with. *+ multiple occurs after.*

A strength of Schaffer and Emerson' study is that it has external validity.

Most of the observations (not stranger anxiety) were made by parents during ordinary activities and reported to researchers.	So the behaviour of the babies was unlikely to be affected by the presence of observers.	It is highly likely that the participants behaved naturally while being observed.

(in own homes)

✗ All glasgow, working class. some years
✓ SAMPLE SIZE: 60+ & lots of data on each.

Another strength of the study is that it was carried out longitudinally.

This means that the same children were followed-up and observed regularly.	The quicker alternative would have been to observe different children at each age. This is called **cross-sectional** design.	But longitudinal designs have better **internal validity** because they do not have the **confounding variable** of individual differences between participants (*participant variables*).

There may also be a problem with how multiple attachment is assessed.

Just because a baby gets distressed when an individual leaves the room does not necessarily mean that the individual is a 'true' attachment figure.	Bowlby (1969) pointed out that children may be distressed when a playmate leaves the room, but this does not signify attachment to them.	So Schaffer and Emerson's view of stages does not distinguish between behaviour shown towards secondary attachment figures and towards playmates.

+ individual differences develop @ diff' rates!

A broader limitation is that there is a problem in studying the asocial year.

Schaffer and Emerson describe the first few weeks as the 'asocial' stage, although important interactions take place.	But young babies have poor coordination and are fairly immobile, making it difficult to make judgments based on observations of their behaviour.	It may be the babies are actually quite social but, because of flawed methods they appear to be asocial.

Evidence on the timing of multiple attachments is conflicting.

Bowlby (1969) argues that most (or all) babies form attachments to a single main carer before they are able to develop multiple attachments.	But multiple attachments appear from the outset in cultures where multiple attachments are the norm (based on research by van Ijzendoorn 1993).	Such cultures are called **collectivist** because families work together jointly in everything (e.g. producing food and raising children).

∴ culturally relative.

These ears demean us both.

KNOWLEDGE CHECK

1. Explain what is meant by the term 'multiple attachments'.
   (2 marks)
2. Outline Schaffer's stages of attachment. *(6 marks)*
3. Explain **two** criticisms of Schaffer's stages of attachment. *(3 marks + 3 marks)*
4. Outline research into multiple attachments. *(6 marks)*
5. Discuss the stages of attachment identified by Schaffer.
   (12 marks AS, 16 marks AL)
6. Describe and evaluate research into multiple attachments.
   (12 marks AS, 16 marks AL)

Animal studies of attachment

Spec spotlight

Animal studies of attachment:
Lorenz and Harlow.

For fans of goslings everywhere.

REVISION BOOSTER

This topic illustrates the importance of thorough revision. That's because you may have to write about any of these: Harlow's animal research only; Lorenz's animal research only; both Harlow's and Lorenz's research; animal research into attachment in general. Don't be tempted to gamble with your revision and leave gaps. Be clear in your own mind about what you will include for each possibility.

Key Study 1: Lorenz (1952) Imprinting

PROCEDURE

Konrad Lorenz randomly divided 12 goose eggs, half hatched with the mother goose in their natural environment and the other half hatched in an incubator where the first moving object they saw was Lorenz.

Mixed all goslings together to see whom they would follow.

Lorenz also observed birds and their later courtship behaviour.

FINDINGS AND CONCLUSIONS

Incubator group followed Lorenz, **control group** followed the mother.

Lorenz identified a *critical period* in which *imprinting* needs to take place, e.g. few hours after hatching. If imprinting did not occur within that time, chicks did not attach themselves to the mother figure.

Sexual imprinting also occurs whereby the birds acquire a template of the desirable characteristics required in a mate.

Key Study 2: Harlow (1958) Importance of contact comfort

PROCEDURE

Harry Harlow reared 16 rhesus monkeys with two wire model 'mothers' (see picture below left):

- In one condition, milk was dispensed by the plain wire 'mother'.
- In a second condition, it was dispensed by the cloth-covered 'mothers'.

The monkeys' preferences were measured.

As a further measure of attachment-like behaviour, the reactions of the monkeys to more frightening situations were observed. For example, Harlow placed the monkeys in novel situations with novel objects. He also added a noisemaking teddy bear to the environment.

Harlow and his colleagues also continued to study the monkeys who had been deprived of their 'real' mother into adulthood.

FINDINGS AND CONCLUSIONS

Baby monkeys cuddled the soft object in preference to the wire one and regardless of which dispensed milk. This suggests that contact comfort was of more importance than food when it came to attachment behaviour.

The monkeys sought comfort from the cloth wire mother when frightened.

As adults, the monkeys that had been deprived of their real mothers suffered severe consequences: they were more aggressive, less sociable and less skilled in mating than other monkeys. They also neglected and sometimes killed their own offspring.

One limitation is generalising findings and conclusions from birds to humans.

The mammalian attachment system is quite different from that in birds.	For example, mammalian mothers show more emotional attachment to their young.	This means that it is not appropriate to generalise Lorenz's ideas to humans.

A strength is support for the concept of imprinting.

Guiton (1966) found that chicks imprinted on yellow washing up gloves would try to mate with them as adults.	This suggests that young animals are born with an innate mechanism to imprint on a moving object present in the critical window of development.	This suggests there is an innate mechanism causing a young animal to imprint on a moving object during in the critical period of development.

Some of Lorenz's observations and conclusions have been questioned.

Guiton (1966) found that chickens imprinted on yellow washing-up gloves tried to mate with them as adults.	But with experience they learned to mate with their own kind.	This study suggests that the effects of imprinting are not as long-lasting as Lorenz believed.

A strength is that Harlow's research has important practical applications.

It has helped social workers understand risk factors in child abuse and so intervene to prevent it (Howe 1998).	We also now understand the importance of attachment figures for baby monkeys in zoos and breeding programmes in the wild.	The usefulness of Harlow's research increases its value.

Harlow faced severe criticism for the ethics of his research.

Rhesus monkeys are similar enough to humans for us to generalise findings, which also means their suffering was presumably human-like.	Harlow himself was aware of the suffering caused. He referred to the wire mothers as 'iron maidens', named after a medieval torture device.	The counter-argument is that Harlow's research was sufficiently important to justify the procedures.

A limitation is generalising from monkeys to humans.

Although monkeys are clearly more similar to humans than Lorenz's geese, they are not humans.	For example, human babies develop speech-like communication ('babbling'). This may influence the formation of attachments.	Psychologists disagree on the extent to which studies of non-human primates can be generalised to humans.

Well hello, lover...

A film called Winged Migration *was made using Canada geese (and other bird species). Human handlers wore high-visibility jackets and made goose-like honking noises. The goslings followed them around almost immediately after they hatched.*

Use Lorenz's research to explain why the goslings behaved in this way.

Rhesus monkeys

KNOWLEDGE CHECK

1. Describe the findings and procedures of **one** animal study of attachment. *(6 marks)*
2. Describe Lorenz's animal studies of attachment. Refer in your answer to what he did and what he found. *(6 marks)*
3. Briefly evaluate either Lorenz's or Harlow's animal studies of attachment. *(4 marks)*
4. Outline and evaluate **two** animal studies of attachment. *(12 marks AS, 16 marks AL)*

Explanations of attachment: Learning theory

Spec spotlight

Explanations of attachment: learning theory.

'Learning theory' is explained on page 72. It is the theory proposed by behaviourists (the behavioural approach).

Classical conditioning of attachment

Unconditioned stimulus		Unconditioned response
Food	→	Pleasure

Neutral stimulus		No response
Caregiver	→	

Unconditioned + neutral stimulus		Unconditioned response
Food + Caregiver	→	Pleasure

Conditioned stimulus		Conditioned response
Caregiver	→	Pleasure

REVISION BOOSTER

Never fall into the trap of writing in general terms about learning theory (e.g. a non-specific description of classical conditioning). In the case of attachment, you have to apply learning theory to explain the development of infant–caregiver attachment.

The general rule is this: if you don't mention attachment throughout your answer then your answer is likely to gain very little credit.

Dollard and Miller (1950) Learning theory of attachment

Importance of food.	This is sometimes called the 'cupboard love' explanation because it emphasises the importance of food in attachment formation. Children learn to love whoever feeds them.
Role of **classical conditioning**.	Classical conditioning involves learning to associate two stimuli. In attachment: **UCS** (food) leads to **UCR** (a feeling of pleasure). This response is not learned so it is an unconditioned response.
Baby learns that mother produces a sense of pleasure.	A caregiver (e.g. mother) starts as a **NS**, i.e. a thing that produces a neutral response. This person providing food over time becomes associated with 'food'. So the neutral stimulus becomes a **CS**. Once conditioning has taken place the sight of the caregiver produces a **CR** of pleasure. According to a learning theorist, this is the basis of attachment love.
Role of **operant conditioning**.	Operant conditioning explains why babies cry for comfort (an important building block for attachment). Crying leads to a response from the caregiver (e.g. feeding). As long as the caregiver provides the correct response, crying is reinforced because it produces a pleasurable consequence.
Negative reinforcement.	At the same time as the baby is reinforced for crying, the caregiver receives *negative reinforcement* because the crying stops (negative reinforcement is escaping from something unpleasant, which is reinforcing). This interplay of positive/negative reinforcement strengthens an attachment.
Drive reduction.	Hunger is a *primary drive*, an innate biological motivator. We are motivated to eat to reduce the hunger drive. Attachment is a *secondary drive* learned by an association between the caregiver and the satisfaction of a primary drive. Sears *et al.* (1957) suggested that, as caregivers provide food, the primary drive of hunger becomes **generalised** to them.

Animal studies provide evidence against food as the basis of attachment.

Lorenz's imprinted geese imprinted maintained attachments regardless of who fed them. Harlow's monkeys attached to a soft surrogate in preference to a wire one with milk.

In both these animal studies, attachment did not develop as a result of feeding.

The same must be true for humans (that food does not create the attachment bond). After all, learning theorists believe that non-human animals and humans are equivalent.

Human research also shows that feeding is not an important factor.

Schaffer and Emerson (1964) showed that for many babies a primary attachment was not to the person who fed them.

This shows that feeding is not the key element to attachment and so there is no unconditioned stimulus or primary drive involved.

The evidence suggests that other factors are more important than food in the formation of attachment.

Cupboard love. Actually that looks more like a wardrobe.

A limitation is that learning theory ignores other factors linked with attachment.

Research shows that quality of attachment is associated with developing reciprocity and good levels of interactional synchrony.

Studies also show that the best quality attachments are with sensitive carers who pick up infant signals and respond appropriately.

It is very hard to reconcile these findings with the idea that attachment develops primarily through feeding.

A strength is that some elements of conditioning could still be involved.

The main problem with learning theory is the idea that feeding provides the unconditioned stimulus, reinforcement or primary drive.

However, many aspects of human development are affected by conditioning so it seems plausible that it could still play a role in attachment (but not in relation to feeding).

For example, associations (classical conditioning) between the primary caregiver and provision of comfort and social interaction could be part of what builds attachment.

Apply it

Margarita is four weeks old and her mum Yvette is her primary caregiver. Yvette prefers to be the one to wake up in the night and feed Margarita, as well as at all other times of the day because she's on maternity leave from work. Margarita's dad Aaron spends just as much time with her, doing the fun stuff like playing. But he's worried that his attachment bond with Margarita won't be as secure as Yvette's.

Look at all of the evidence on this spread. Explain in terms of learning theory why Aaron is concerned. What would you say to him to address his concerns?

There is a newer learning explanation based on social learning theory (SLT).

Hay and Vespo (1988) suggest that parents teach children to love them by *modelling* attachment behaviours (e.g. hugging them and other family members).

And also by rewarding them with approval when they display their own attachment behaviours ('that's a lovely smile', etc.).

In this version, babies have learned attachment behaviours as a result of their interactions, which fits with research on the importance of interactional synchrony and reciprocity (see page 48).

KNOWLEDGE CHECK

1. Describe the learning theory explanation of attachment.
   (4 marks)
2. Outline **two** criticisms of the learning theory explanation of attachment.
   (3 marks + 3 marks)
3. Discuss learning theory as an explanation of attachment.
   (12 marks AS, 16 marks AL)

Explanations of attachment: Bowlby's theory

Spec spotlight

Explanations of attachment: Bowlby's monotropic theory.

The concepts of a critical period and an internal working model.

REVISION BOOSTER

Bowlby's theory often provokes strong feelings because it touches on the issue of who is best equipped to look after babies (i.e. is it always the mother?).

It's perfectly OK for you to have strong opinions on this (and any) issue. But don't allow your personal beliefs to colour your judgement when writing about Bowlby's theory. It's not acceptable to say, 'Bowlby was a sexist pig because he believed that a woman's place is in the home'. But it is acceptable (highly desirable in fact) to criticise his theory rationally in terms of the evidence.

Most infants form attachments with several caregivers – although they don't usually have a shared dress code.

Bowlby's (1958, 1969) monotropic theory of attachment

Attachment is innate, like imprinting.	Bowlby gave an evolutionary explanation: that attachment is an innate system that gives a survival advantage. Imprinting and attachment evolved because they ensure young animals stay close to their caregivers and this protects them from hazards.
Monotropic = a *primary attachment figure*.	Bowlby's theory is described as monotropic because of the emphasis on the child's attachment to one caregiver (mono = 'one' and tropic = 'leaning towards'). This attachment is different from others and more important.
More time spent with the mother-figure is beneficial.	Bowlby believed that the more time a baby spent with this *primary attachment figure* / mother-figure (not necessarily the biological mother) the better. There are two main reasons: (1) *Law of continuity* – the more constant a child's care, the better the quality of attachment. (2) *Law of accumulated separation* – the effects of every separation add up. So, 'the safest dose is therefore a zero dose'.
Babies are born with *social releasers*.	Bowlby suggested that babies are born with a set of innate 'cute' behaviours (e.g. smiling, cooing, gripping) that encourage attention from adults. The purpose of these social releasers is to activate the adult attachment system (i.e. make an adult feel love towards the baby); Bowlby recognised that attachment is a reciprocal system.
There is a *critical period*.	Bowlby proposed that there is a critical period of about two years when the infant attachment system is active. In fact, he viewed this as more of a *sensitive period*. A child is maximally sensitive up to the age of two years. If an attachment has not formed in this time, he or she will find it much harder to form one later.
The first attachment forms an *internal working model* of relationships.	Bowlby argued that the child forms a mental representation (internal working model) of the relationship with their primary attachment figure. This internal working model serves as a 'template' for what relationships are like. A child whose first experience is a loving relationship with a reliable caregiver will tend to form an expectation that all relationships are loving and reliable. However, a child whose first relationship involves poor treatment may expect such treatment from others. The internal working model may also affect the child's later ability to be a parent themselves.

The evidence for monotropy is mixed.

Schaffer and Emerson (1964) found that most babies did attach to one person at first, but a significant minority formed multiple attachments at the same time.

This contradicts Bowlby's assertion that babies form one attachment to a primary caregiver and that this attachment is unique.

Attachment to mothers (not fathers) better predicts later behaviour, but this may be because mother is the primary attachment, not the different attachment quality.

There is clear evidence to support the existence and value of social releasers.

Brazleton et al. (1975) instructed primary attachment figures to ignore their babies' social releasers (cute infant behaviours).

Babies (who were previously shown to be normally responsive) initially showed some distress, but eventually some curled up and lay motionless.

This supports Bowlby's ideas about the significance of infant social behaviour eliciting caregiving from adults and the role of releasers in initiating social interaction.

There is also support for the idea of an internal working model.

The idea of internal working models predicts that patterns of attachment will be passed from one generation to the next.

Bailey et al. (2007) studied 99 mothers; those with poor attachment to own parents were more likely to have one-year-olds who were poorly attached.

This supports Bowlby's idea of an internal working model of attachment as it is being passed through families.

Monotropy is socially sensitive because of implications for mothers' lifestyle.

The law of accumulated separation states that having substantial time apart from a primary attachment figure risks a poor quality attachment that will disadvantage the child in a range of ways.

Feminists (e.g. Burman 1994) argue that mothers are blamed for anything that goes wrong in a child's life and pushes mothers into making lifestyle choices, e.g. not returning to work when a child is born.

However, this was not Bowlby's intention. He saw himself as boosting the status of mothers by emphasising the importance of their role.

A limitation is Bowlby may have overemphasised the role of attachment.

An alternative explanation is that the child's *temperament* (the child's genetically influenced personality) is important in the development of social behaviour.

Temperament researchers suggest that some babies are more anxious and some more sociable than others as a result of their genetic make-up (Kagan 1982).

Temperamental differences rather than quality of attachment can explain later social behaviour.

Apply it

Eddie is six months old. His mum died not long after he was born and his dad is his primary caregiver who takes good care of all his needs.

Camelia is 18 months old. She has always lived in an orphanage where 'care' is provided by several different staff members. New staff come and go on a regular basis.

Leah is four years old. She was physically abused by her biological parents for the first two years of her life, but is now being adopted into a very caring and loving home.

Use Bowlby's theory and the concepts described on this spread to explain the quality of attachments you would expect to find in these three cases.

Which of Eddie, Camelia and Leah do you predict is most likely to go on to be a successful parent themselves? Explain your choice.

KNOWLEDGE CHECK

1. In relation to attachment, explain what is meant by the terms 'critical period' and 'internal working model'.
   (2 marks + 2 marks)
2. Outline Bowlby's monotropic theory of attachment.   *(6 marks)*
3. Briefly evaluate Bowlby's theory of attachment.   *(4 marks)*
4. Discuss Bowlby's theory of attachment.
   (12 marks AS, 16 marks AL)

Ainsworth's Strange Situation

Spec spotlight

Ainsworth's Strange Situation.

Types of attachment: secure, insecure–avoidant and insecure–resistant.

A dog playing a violin – now that's what I call a strange situation.

Apply it

Nell likes to be with her mum but is happy to play elsewhere in the room. However, she does keep one eye on where her mum is, and gets a bit upset if her mum is out of the room for a long time.

Sunny clings to his mum a lot and likes to be carried around. His mum finds it difficult to put Sunny down for any length of time without him becoming distressed.

Gennady doesn't seem to mind whether his mum is there or not. He hardly notices if she leaves the room, and he doesn't show any inclination to be with her when she returns.

Identify each baby's attachment type and explain your decisions. What other behaviours would you expect to observe in each baby?

Key Study: Ainsworth (1969) The Strange Situation

PROCEDURE

Mary Ainsworth (1969) developed the Strange Situation as a method to assess the quality of a child's attachment to a caregiver.

It is a *controlled observation* procedure in a lab (a controlled environment) with a two-way mirror through which psychologists can observe an infant's behaviour.

Five categories are used to judge attachment quality:

1. Proximity seeking: well-attached infants stay close to caregiver.
2. Exploration and secure-base behaviour: good attachment makes a child confident to explore, using the caregiver as point of safety.
3. Stranger anxiety: displayed by well-attached infants.
4. Separation anxiety: displayed by well-attached infants.
5. Response to reunion with the caregiver after separation for a short period of time: well-attached infants are enthusiastic.

The procedure has seven 'episodes', each lasting three minutes.

1. The child is encouraged to explore by caregiver.
2. Stranger enters and talks to caregiver.
3. Caregiver leaves.
4. The caregiver returns, the stranger leaves.
5. The caregiver leaves the child alone.
6. The stranger returns.
7. The caregiver returns.

FINDINGS AND CONCLUSIONS

Ainsworth found distinct patterns in the way infants behaved. She identified three main types of attachment.

Secure attachment (Type B: 60–75% of British toddlers):

- Child happy to explore but seeks proximity with caregiver (secure base).
- Shows moderate separation anxiety and stranger anxiety.
- Requires and accepts comfort from caregiver on reunion.

Insecure–avoidant attachment (Type A: 20–25% of British toddlers):

- Child explores freely but does not seek proximity (no secure base).
- Shows little/no separation and stranger anxiety.
- Does not require comfort at the reunion stage.

Insecure–resistant attachment (Type C: 3% of British toddlers):

- Child explores less and seeks greater proximity.
- Shows considerable stranger and separation anxiety.
- Resists comfort when reunited with caregiver.

There is predictive validity of attachment types in the Strange Situation.

Attachment type predicts later development. For example, secure babies typically have greater success at school and more lasting romantic relationships.

In contrast, insecure–resistant attachment is associated with the worst outcomes, e.g. bullying (Kokkinos 2007) and adult mental health problems (Ward et al. 2006).

This is evidence for the validity of the concept because it can explain future outcomes.

A strength is that the Strange Situation shows very good inter-rater reliability.

Different observers watching the same children generally agree on attachment type. Bick et al. (2012) found 94% agreement in one team.

This may be because the Strange Situation takes place under controlled conditions and because the behavioural categories are easy to observe.

So we can be confident that the attachment type of an infant identified in the Strange Situation does not just depend on who is observing them.

A limitation is that the Strange Situation may be a culture-bound test.

The test might not have the same meaning in countries outside Western Europe and the USA.

Cultural differences in children's experiences mean they respond differently.

Also caregivers from different cultures behave differently.

Takahashi (1990) notes that Japanese mothers are rarely separated from infants, thus the infants show high levels of separation anxiety.

Another limitation is that temperament may be a confounding variable.

Ainsworth assumed that the main influence on separation and stranger anxiety was the quality of the attachment.

But Kagan (1982) suggests that temperament (the child's genetically influenced personality) is a more important influence on behaviour in the Strange Situation.

This challenges the validity of the Strange Situation because its intention is to measure the quality of attachment, not the temperament of the child (i.e. a confounding variable).

A limitation is that there may be other attachment types.

Ainsworth identified three attachment types: insecure–avoidant (A), secure (B), and insecure–resistant (C).

Main and Solomon (1986) pointed out that some children display atypical attachments that do not fit types A, B or C. This is disorganised attachment – a mix of avoidant and resistant behaviours.

This challenges Ainsworth's initial notion of attachment types and could question whether the Strange Situation is a useful method to identify these types.

'Are you not getting this mother?! I am insecure-resistant!!'

KNOWLEDGE CHECK

1. In relation to attachment, explain what is meant by the terms 'secure', 'insecure–avoidant' and 'insecure–resistant'.
    (2 marks + 2 marks + 2 marks)
2. Ainsworth identified three types of attachment. Choose any **two** types and explain **one** difference between them. *(2 marks)*
3. Outline Ainsworth's Strange Situation. *(6 marks)*
4. Give **one or more** criticisms of Ainsworth's Strange Situation. *(4 marks)*
5. Describe and evaluate research into types of attachment.
    (12 marks AS, 16 marks AL)

Cultural variations in attachment

Spec spotlight

Cultural variations in attachment including van Ijzendoorn.

'I just need to learn the study by van Iz....van Izen..van Oozen.. van Izling... aw – I give up'.

Psychology student Neville wasn't renowned for his cultural sensitivity.

REVISION BOOSTER

In an exam question you may have to describe the procedures and findings of studies, or just one of them. For example, van Ijzendoorn is specifically mentioned in the specification, so you need to be thoroughly familiar with all aspects of what he did and what he found in his research.

Alternatively, you might have to write about 'research', a term which gives you more flexibility because it doesn't tie you to one specific study or aspect of a study (and can even include theories, if there are any relevant to the topic).

Key Study 1: van Ijzendoorn and Kroonenberg (1988) Meta-analysis

PROCEDURE

The researchers looked at the proportions of secure, insecure–avoidant and insecure–resistant attachments across a range of countries.

They also looked at the differences within the same countries to get an idea of variations within a culture.

They found 32 studies of attachment where the Strange Situation had been used. These were conducted in eight countries, 15 in the USA. Overall the studies yielded results for 1,990 children.

The data were **meta-analysed**, results being combined and weighted for sample size.

FINDINGS AND CONCLUSIONS

Secure attachment was the most common classification in all countries, but ranged from 50% in China to 75% in Britain.

In **individualist** cultures rates of *insecure–resistant attachment* were similar to Ainsworth's original sample (all under 14%) but this was not true for the **collectivist** samples from China, Japan and Israel where rates were above 25% (and where rates of *insecure–avoidant attachment* were reduced).

This suggests that there were cultural differences in the distribution of insecure attachment.

Variations between results of studies *within* the same country were actually 150% greater than those *between* countries.

In the USA, one study found 46% securely attached compared to one sample as high as 90%.

Key Study 2: Simonelli et al. (2014) An Italian key study

PROCEDURE

These researchers assessed 76 12-month olds using the Strange Situation to see whether the proportion of attachment types still matched previous studies in Italy.

Mothers were reasonably varied in terms of their education levels (57% university degree, 40% high school, 2% did not finish high school) and their professions (48% employees, 13% professionals, 39% did not work or worked part-time).

FINDINGS AND CONCLUSIONS

Simonelli et al. found that 50% were secure, with 36% insecure–avoidant. This was a lower rate of secure attachment than found in previous studies.

The researchers suggested this was due to the increasing numbers of mothers working long hours and using professional childcare. Cultural changes can make dramatic differences in the patterns of attachment.

A strength of meta-analysis is that you can end up with very large samples.

In van Ijzendoorn and Kroonenberg's meta-analysis there was a total of nearly 2000 babies and their primary attachment figures.

Even Simonelli *et al.*'s study had large comparison groups from previous research, although their own samples were smaller.

This is a strength because large samples increase **internal validity** by reducing the impact of biased methodology or very unusual participants.

A limitation is that the samples used may not be representative of cultures.

Van Ijzendoorn and Kroonenberg's meta-analysis made comparisons between countries, not cultures. Within any country there are different cultures each with different child-rearing practices.

For example, van Ijzendoorn and Sagi (2001) found attachment types in urban Tokyo in similar proportions to Western studies. A more rural sample over-represented insecure–resistant individuals.

This means that comparisons between countries (such as Italy or Korea) may have little meaning. The particular cultural characteristics (and thus caregiving styles) of the sample need to be specified.

The Strange Situation method may be biased towards American/British culture.

The Strange Situation was designed by an American researcher (Ainsworth) based on a British theory (Bowlby). This theory and assessment may not be applicable to other cultures.

Trying to apply a theory or technique designed for one culture to another is known as imposed etic (etic means cultural universals) which disregards the notion of cultural emic (cultural uniqueness).

The idea that a lack of pleasure on reunion indicates insecure attachment is an imposed etic. In Germany this behaviour might be seen more as independence than avoidance and not a sign of insecurity.

There is an alternative explanation for the similarities found between cultures.

Bowlby's explanation for cultural similarities was that attachment is innate and universal so produces the same kind of behaviours all over the world.

Van Ijzendoorn and Kroonenberg proposed an alternative possibility. They suggest that small cross-cultural differences may reflect the effects of the mass media.

Many books and TV programmes are broadcast around the world and create parenting norms, so similarities in child-rearing have become more common.

Temperament may be a confounding variable in the Strange Situation.

Ainsworth assumed that the main influence on separation and stranger anxiety was the quality of the attachment.

Kagan (1982) suggests that temperament (the genetic personality of the child) is a more important influence on behaviour in the Strange Situation.

The Strange Situation may actually be measuring genetic differences in temperament between cultures rather than attachment/parenting style.

Apply it

Yanyu was born in China and came to Britain to go to university. She married Frank and they have a baby called Billy. They recently visited Yanyu's parents in China. Her mum was worried because she felt that Yanyu and Billy didn't have a very close bond. For example, she expected Billy to spend more time close to Yanyu and be a bit more upset when Yanyu left the room.

Using psychological research, explain how Yanyu could reassure her mum about the quality of her attachment with Billy.

Oh dear, someone's not happy... The Strange Situation may simply be measuring the child's temperament rather than parenting style.

KNOWLEDGE CHECK

1. In relation to attachment, explain what is meant by the term 'cultural variations'.
   (2 marks)
2. Outline van Ijzendoorn's research into cultural variations in attachment.
   (4 marks)
3. Describe the procedures of **one** study into cultural variations in attachment.
   (4 marks)
4. Outline what research has found out about cultural variations in attachment.
   (4 marks)
5. Describe and evaluate research into cultural variations in attachment.
   (12 marks AS, 16 marks AL)

Bowlby's theory of maternal deprivation

Spec spotlight

Bowlby's theory of maternal deprivation.

'What's your problem? You never seen anyone who's glued themselves to a wall before?'

REVISION BOOSTER

There is some overlap between topics within this chapter.

Research into the effects of institutionalisation on Romanian orphans (next spread) is relevant to Bowlby's theory of maternal deprivation. You can use this as an AO3 point. The key is to make your evaluation effective by explaining what the research tells us about Bowlby's theory, not by describing the research itself (that wouldn't be relevant).

Bowlby's (1951) Theory of maternal deprivation

Continued emotional care from mother is essential.	Continuous emotional (maternal) care from a mother or mother-substitute is necessary for normal emotional and intellectual development.
Separation from mother may lead to *maternal deprivation.*	Bowlby believed that mother-love in infancy is 'as important for mental health as vitamins and proteins are for physical health'.
Separation is different from deprivation.	• Separation means the child not being physically in the presence of the primary attachment figure. • Deprivation means losing emotional care as a result of the separation. Deprivation can be avoided if alternative emotional care is offered, thus separation doesn't always cause deprivation.
Critical period of 30 months.	If a child is separated from their mother (without substitute emotional care) for an extended time during the first 30 months, then psychological damage is inevitable.
Intellectual development: deprivation lowers IQ.	If a child is deprived of maternal care for too long during the critical period they will suffer mental retardation and abnormally low IQ. Goldfarb (1947) found lower IQs in children from institutions compared to fostered children.
Emotional development: deprivation linked to *affectionless psychopathy.*	Lack of emotional care may also lead to affectionless psychopathy – the inability to experience guilt or strong emotion for others. This prevents the person developing normal relationships and is associated with criminality.

Key study: Bowlby (1944) 44 thieves study

PROCEDURE	The sample in this study was 44 delinquent teenagers accused of stealing. Families were also interviewed to establish any prolonged separations from mothers.
	All 'thieves' were interviewed for signs of affectionless psychopathy: characterised by a lack of affection, guilt and empathy.
FINDINGS AND CONCLUSIONS	14 of the 44 thieves could be described as affectionless psychopaths. Of these, 12 had experienced prolonged separation from their mothers in the first two years of their lives.
	In contrast only 5 of the remaining 30 'thieves' had experienced separations. This suggests prolonged early separation/deprivation caused affectionless psychopathy.

A limitation is that sources of evidence for maternal deprivation are flawed.

Goldfarb (see facing page) studied war-orphans who were traumatised and often had poor after-care. These factors may have caused later developmental difficulties rather than separation.

Similarly, children growing up from birth in poor quality institutions were deprived of many aspects of care, not just maternal care.

Bowlby carried out the assessments for affectionless psychopathy and the family interviews himself, knowing what he hoped to find. This may have produced biased results.

There is also counter-evidence which does not support Bowlby's findings.

Lewis (1954) partially **replicated** the 44 thieves study on a larger scale, looking at 500 young people.

Early prolonged maternal separation did not predict criminality or difficulty forming close relationships.

This is a limitation of Bowlby's theory because it suggests that other factors may affect the outcome of early maternal separation.

Later research suggests that the critical period is more of a sensitive period.

Koluchová's (1976) **case study** of Czech twin boys isolated from age 18 months (locked in a cupboard). Later they were looked after by two loving adults and appeared to recover fully.

Shows that severe deprivation can have positive outcomes provided the child has some social interaction and good aftercare.

Cases like the Czech twins show that the period identified by Bowlby may be a 'sensitive' one but it cannot be critical.

A strength is that animal studies have demonstrated maternal deprivation.

Most psychologists are critical of the maternal deprivation theory, but one line of research supports the idea that maternal deprivation can have long-term effects.

Levy *et al.* (2003) showed that separating baby rats from their mother for as a little as a day had a permanent effect on social development.

However, there is always some doubt over the extent to which animal studies like this can be **generalised** to human behaviour.

A limitation is that Bowlby didn't distinguish between deprivation and privation.

Rutter (1981) distinguished between deprivation (the loss of the primary attachment figure after attachment has developed) and privation (the failure to form any attachment at all).

Rutter argues that the severe long-term damage Bowlby associated with deprivation is actually more likely to be the result of privation.

Many of the 44 thieves in Bowlby's study had moved from home to home during their childhood so may have never formed attachments in the first place. This could be the cause of their affectionless psychopathy rather than deprivation.

Apply it

Harold Skeels and Harold Dye (1939) studied two groups of 1–2-year-old orphaned children. One group was raised in a home for 'mentally retarded' teenage girls and given one-to-one care (by the girls). The other group remained in an unstimulating orphanage without individual care. The children's intelligence (IQ) was tested at the start and the end of an 18-month period. The mean IQ of the one-to-one children had increased from 64.3 to 91.8 points. But in the orphanage children, the mean IQ decreased from 86.7 to 60.5 points.

Use Bowlby's theory of maternal deprivation to explain Skeels and Dye's results.

Bowlby thought that mother and infant should not be separated – even during business hours.

KNOWLEDGE CHECK

1. Explain what is meant by the term 'maternal deprivation'. *(2 marks)*
2. Outline Bowlby's theory of maternal deprivation. *(4 marks)*
3. Explain **two** criticisms of Bowlby's theory of maternal deprivation. *(3 marks + 3 marks)*
4. Outline **one** study that supports Bowlby's theory of maternal deprivation. In your answer include details of what the researcher(s) did and what they found. *(6 marks)*
5. Describe and evaluate Bowlby's theory of maternal deprivation. *(12 marks AS, 16 marks AL)*

Romanian orphan studies

Spec spotlight

Romanian orphan studies: effects of institutionalisation.

Institutionalised Romanian orphans. No joke.

Tatiana began life in a Romanian orphanage but was adopted into a British family when she was one year old. Now aged six years, she is being referred to an educational psychologist for two main reasons. Her performance at school is very poor, her reading and writing in particular – she finds even the basics difficult.

She also has serious behavioural problems, especially extreme attention-seeking – she is 'clingy' with everyone, even complete strangers.

Explain why Tatiana might be behaving in these ways. Refer to psychological research in your explanation.

Effects of institutionalisation

Disinhibited attachment.	The child is equally friendly and affectionate towards people they know well or who are strangers. This may be an adaptation to multiple caregivers.
Damage to intellectual development.	Institutionalised children often show signs of mental retardation. This effect is not as pronounced if the children are adopted before 6 months of age.

Key study: Rutter *et al.* (2011) English and Romanian adoptee study

PROCEDURE

The researchers have followed a group of 165 Romanian orphans who experienced very poor conditions before being adopted in Britain.

This **longitudinal** study has tested the extent to which good care can make up for poor early experiences in institutions. Physical, **cognitive** and emotional development has been assessed at 4, 6, 11 and 15 years.

The study also followed a **control group** of 52 adopted British children.

FINDINGS AND CONCLUSIONS

Half of the orphans showed mental retardation when they came to the UK. At age 11 recovery rates were related to their age of adoption:
- Those adopted before six months had a mean IQ of 102.
- Those adopted between six months and two years had a mean IQ of 86.
- Those adopted after two years had a mean IQ of 77.

Frequency of *disinhibited attachment* related to the age of adoption.
- Apparent in children adopted after they were six months old: clinginess, attention-seeking and indiscriminate affection to strangers.
- Rare in children adopted before the age of six months.

These findings support the view that there is a *sensitive period* in the development of attachments – a failure to form an attachment before the age of six months appears to have long-lasting effects.

Zeanah *et al.* (2005) Bucharest Early Intervention Project

PROCEDURE

The researchers used the Strange Situation to assess attachment in 95 children aged 12–31 months who had spent most of their lives in institutional care.

They were compared to a control group of 50 children who had never experienced institutional care.

FINDINGS AND CONCLUSIONS

Only 19% of the institutionalised group were securely attached.

65% classified with *disorganised attachment*.

Studying Romanian orphans has important practical applications.

Results from this research have led to improvements in the way children are cared for in institutions (Langton 2006).

Children's homes now avoid having large numbers of caregivers for each child. They have one or two 'key workers' who play a central role.

This gives the child a chance to develop normal attachments and avoid disinhibited attachments, immensely valuable in practical terms.

Romanian orphan study has fewer confounding variables than other research.

There were many orphan studies before the Romanian orphans became available to study. These often involved children who experienced loss or trauma before they were institutionalised.

Neglect, abuse and bereavement meant it was hard to observe the effects of institutionalisation in isolation. The children were affected by multiple factors functioning as confounding variables.

In the case of Romanian orphans it is possible to study institutionalisation without these confounding variables because most were abandoned at birth. So the findings have increased **internal validity**.

However, there may be issues with generalisability in Romanian studies.

The conditions of the orphanages are so bad that the results may not apply to institutional care or general situations of deprivation.

Romanian orphanages had particularly poor standards of care, especially when it came to forming any relationship with the children.

The unusual situational variables mean the studies may lack generalisability.

A limitation is that children were not randomly assigned to conditions.

Rutter *et al.* did not interfere with the adoption process, so those children adopted early may have been more sociable ones, a confounding variable.

To control for such variables, the *Bucharest Early Intervention* study (see facing page) did randomly assign the orphans to institutional care or fostering.

This is methodologically better because it removes the confounding variable of some children being selected by parents, but it raises ethical issues.

The long-term effects of early experience are not yet clear.

It is too soon to say for certain whether children suffered short- or long-term effects because the adopted orphans have only been followed into their mid-teens.

The children who spent longer in institutions and currently lag behind in intellectual development or display attachment difficulties may still 'catch up' as adults.

Equally, early-adopted/fostered children who appear to have no issues now may experience emotional problems as adults.

KNOWLEDGE CHECK

1. Explain what is meant by the term 'institutionalisation'.
   (2 marks)

2. Describe the procedures and findings of **one** Romanian orphan study. *(6 marks)*

3. Outline research into the effects of institutionalisation. Refer in your answer to what the researcher(s) did and what they found. *(6 marks)*

4. Discuss research into the effects of institutionalisation.
   (12 marks AS, 16 marks AL)

Influence of early attachment on later relationships

Spec spotlight

Influence of early attachment on childhood and adult relationships, including the role of an internal working model.

Children who have positive early relationships tend to have successful relationships in later life. Go on then you two – that's probably worth an awkward high five.

Internal working models are discussed on page 58.

Internal working model

First attachment is a template for future relationships.	The quality of a child's first attachment is crucial because it provides a template that will affect the nature of their future relationships. This is due to the influence of the *internal working model* created by that first attachment.
Good experience of attachment = good relationship expectations.	A child whose first experience is of a loving relationship with a reliable caregiver assumes this is how all relationships are meant to be. They will then seek out functional relationships and behave functionally within them.
Bad experience of attachment = bad relationship expectations.	A child with bad experiences of their first attachment will bring these experiences to bear on later relationships. This may mean they struggle to form relationships in the first place or they do not behave appropriately in them.
Secure infants form better friendships and are less likely to bully.	Securely attached infants tend to go on to form the best quality childhood friendships (Kerns 1994). Securely attached infants are less likely to be involved in bullying whereas insecure–avoidant children are most likely to be victims and insecure–resistant are most likely to be bullies (Myron-Wilson and Smith 1998).
Internal working models affect parenting.	People base their parenting style on their internal working model so attachment type tends to be passed on through generations of a family.

All of his life Josh has had trouble forming happy relationships. As a child, he was highly upset whenever his mum left the room, but didn't want to know her when she came back. At school, he bullied other children, typically those he considered weaker than himself. As an adult, Josh has never been able to hold down a romantic relationship, preferring to spend most of his time on his own even when he had a partner.

Using the concept of an internal working model, explain how Josh's problems with relationships could be traced back to his infancy.

Key study: Hazan and Shaver (1987) Romantic relationships

PROCEDURE	The researchers analysed 620 replies to a 'love quiz' printed in an American local newspaper.
	The quiz assessed three different aspects of relationships: • Respondents' current and most important relationship. • General love experiences. • Attachment type.
FINDINGS AND CONCLUSIONS	56% of respondents were identified as *securely attached*, with 25% *insecure–avoidant* and 19% *insecure–resistant*.
	Their attachment type was reflected in their romantic relationships: • *Secure respondents* were the most likely to have good and longer-lasting romantic relationships. • *Avoidant respondents* tended to be jealous and fear intimacy.

A limitation is that the evidence on continuity of attachment is mixed.

Internal working models predict that attachment type in infancy is usually the same as that characterising the person's future relationships.

However, Zimmerman (2000) assessed infant attachment type and adolescent attachments to parents. There was very little relationship between quality of infant and adolescent attachment.

This is a limitation because it is not what we would expect if internal working models were important in development.

A further limitation is that most studies have issues with validity.

Most studies of attachment do not use the Strange Situation but assess infant–parent attachment using interviews or questionnaires, not in infancy but years later.

The validity of questionnaires and interviews is limited because they depend on respondents being honest and having a realistic view of their own relationships.

A related problem concerns the retrospective nature of assessment. Looking back in adulthood at one's early attachment lacks validity because it relies on accurate recollections.

Several studies indicate associations but this is not the same as causation.

There are alternative explanations for the continuity that often exists between infant and later relationships.

The child's temperament may influence both infant attachment and the quality of later relationships.

This is a limitation because it is counter to Bowlby's view that the internal working model caused these outcomes.

The influence of infant attachment on future relationships is exaggerated.

Clarke and Clarke (1998) describe the influence of infant attachment on later relationships as probabilistic.

People are not doomed to always have bad relationships because they had attachment problems. They just have a greater risk of problems.

By over-emphasising this risk we become too pessimistic about people's futures.

There is a theoretical problem with research related to internal working models.

Internal working models are unconscious – we are not directly aware of their influence on us. So we would not really expect to get direct evidence about them through self-report methods which require conscious awareness.

When participants self-report on their relationships they are relying on their conscious understanding of those relationships. At best, self-report gives us indirect evidence about internal working models.

This is a potential limitation of most research involving the concept of internal working models.

Infant–parent attachment may be assessed retrospectively using questionnaires – but responses may not always be truthful.

KNOWLEDGE CHECK

1. Explain what is meant by the term 'internal working model'. *(2 marks)*

2. In relation to the influence of early attachments on later relationships, outline the role of an 'internal working model'. *(6 marks)*

3. Describe **one** study into the influence of early attachments on later relationships. *(6 marks)*

4. Describe and evaluate research into the influence of early attachments on later relationships. Refer in your answer to both childhood and adult relationships. *(12 marks AS, 16 marks AL)*

Origins of psychology

Spec spotlight

Origins of psychology: Wundt, introspection and the emergence of psychology as a science.

If you're not sure what is meant by 'introspection', you need to take a long hard look at yourself.

Apply it

Two students are discussing whether or not psychology can really be considered a science. Tara thinks it can and argues that Wundt made a significant contribution to the development of psychology as a science. Max accepts that behaviourism is quite scientific but reckons that many approaches in psychology are not scientific at all.

Can psychology be regarded as a science? Explain your answer, referring to Tara's and Max's views.

Wundt and introspection

Wilhelm Wundt established the first psychology lab.	Opened in Leipzig, Germany in 1879. The aim was to describe the nature of human consciousness (the 'mind') in a carefully controlled and scientific environment – a lab.
Wundt pioneered the method of introspection.	Introspection was the first systematic experimental attempt to study the mind by breaking up conscious awareness into basic structures of thoughts, images and sensations. Isolating the structure of consciousness in this way is called *structuralism*.
Standardised procedures.	The same standardised instructions were given to all participants. Procedures could be repeated (**replicated**). For instance, participants were given a ticking metronome and they would report their thoughts, images and sensations, which were then recorded.
Significance of Wundt's work.	Although Wundt's early attempt to study the mind would be seen today as naïve, his work was significant as it marked the separation of modern scientific psychology from its broader philosophical roots.

Emergence of psychology as a science

1900s Early **behaviourists** rejected introspection.	John B. Watson (1913) argued that introspection was subjective, in that it varied from person to person. According to the behaviourist approach, 'scientific' psychology should only study phenomena that can be observed and measured.
1930s Behaviourist scientific approach dominated psychology.	B.F. Skinner (1953) brought the language and rigour of the natural sciences into psychology. The behaviourists' focus on learning, and the use of carefully controlled lab studies, would dominate psychology for the next few decades.
1950s **cognitive approach** used scientific procedures to study mental processes.	Following the cognitive revolution of the 1960s, the study of mental processes was seen as legitimate within psychology. Although mental processes remain 'private', cognitive psychologists are able to make *inferences* about how these work on the basis of tests conducted in a controlled environment (lab).
1990s The **biological approach** introduced technological advances.	Biological psychologists have taken advantage of recent advances in technology, including recording brain activity, using scanning techniques such as **fMRI** and **EEG**, and advanced genetic research.

Some aspects of Wundt's methods would be classed as scientific today.

For instance, he recorded the introspections within a controlled lab environment.

He also standardised his procedures so that all participants received the same information and were tested in the same way.

For this reason, Wundt's research can be considered a forerunner to the later scientific approaches in psychology that were to come.

Other aspects of this research would be considered unscientific today.

Wundt relied on participants self-reporting their 'private' mental processes. Such data is subjective and participants may not have wanted to reveal some of the thoughts they were having.

Participants would also not have had exactly the same thoughts every time, so establishing general principles would not have been possible. General laws are useful to predict future behaviour, one of the aims of science.

Wundt's early efforts to study the mind were naïve and would not meet the criteria of scientific enquiry.

A strength is that research in modern psychology can claim to be scientific.

Psychology has the same aims as the natural sciences – to describe, understand, predict and control behaviour.

The **learning approaches**, cognitive approach and biological approach all rely on the use of scientific methods – for example, lab studies to investigate theories in a controlled and unbiased way.

Throughout the 20th century and beyond, psychology has established itself as a scientific discipline.

One problem with psychology is that not all approaches use objective methods.

The **humanistic approach** is anti-scientific and does not attempt to formulate general laws of behaviour. It is concerned only with documenting unique subjective experience.

The **psychodynamic approach** makes use of the **case study** method. This is based on interview techniques which are open to bias, and no attempt is made to gather a representative sample of the population.

For this reason, many claim that a scientific approach to the study of human thought and experience is not possible, nor is it desirable, as there are important differences between the subject matter of psychology and the natural sciences.

I ♥ PSYCHOLOGY

Yes of course you do – but the question of whether psychology is a science is not one that has a straightforward answer...

The learning approach: Behaviourism

Spec spotlight

Learning approaches: The behaviourist approach including classical conditioning and Pavlov's research, operant conditioning, types of reinforcement and Skinner's research.

'Conditioning' means 'learning'.

'Have you heard of a bloke called Ivan Pavlov?'

'I must admit, the name rings a bell.'

Apply it

Joel is addicted to online fruit machine gambling. He spends a lot of time and money on this and other forms of online gambling.

Explain Joel's gambling addiction in terms of operant conditioning. Use the concepts of positive and negative reinforcement in your explanation. Explain a feature of operant conditioning that might lead to a reduction in his gambling behaviour.

Key assumptions of the behaviourist approach

Focus on *observable* behaviour only.	The behaviourist approach is only concerned with studying behaviour that can be observed and measured. It is not concerned with mental processes of the mind. *Introspection* was rejected by behaviourists as its concepts were vague and difficult to measure.	
Controlled lab studies.	Behaviourists tried to maintain more control and objectivity within their research and relied on lab studies to achieve th	
Use of non-human animals.	Behaviourists suggest the processes that govern learning are the same in all species, so animals (e.g. rats, cats, dogs and pigeons) can replace humans as experimental subjects.	
Classical conditioning Pavlov's research.	Learning through association. UCS → UCR NS → no response NS + UCS CS → CR (See examples on pages 56 and 96.)	**Pavlov's research** – conditioning dogs to salivate when a bell rings: *Before conditioning*: **UCS** = food, **UCR** = salivation, **NS** = bell *During conditioning* Bell and food occur at same time. *After conditioning* **CS** = bell, **CR** = salivation Pavlov showed how a neutral stimulu (bell) can come to elicit a new learne response (conditioned response) through association.
Operant conditioning Skinner's research	Learning is an active process whereby humans and animals *operate* on their environment. Behaviour is shaped and maintained by its *consequences*.	**Skinner's research** – rats and pigeons, in specially designed cages (Skinner boxes). When a rat activated a lever (or a pigeon pecked a disc) it was *rewarde* with a food pellet. A desirable consequence led to behaviour being repeated. If pressing a lever meant an animal avoided an electric shock, the behaviour would also be repeated.
Three types of *consequences* of behaviour.	**Positive reinforcement** – receiving a reward when behaviour is performed. **Negative reinforcement** – when an animal or human produces behaviour that avoids something unpleasant. **Punishment** – an unpleasant consequence of behaviour. Positive reinforcement and negative reinforcement increase the likelihood that behaviour will be repeated. Punishment decreases it.	

A strength of behaviourism is that it gave psychology scientific credibility.

The approach focused on the careful measurement of observable behaviour within controlled lab settings.

Behaviourists emphasised the importance of scientific processes such as objectivity and **replication**.

This brought the language and methods of the natural sciences into psychology, giving the subject greater credibility and status.

The laws of learning developed by behaviourists have real-life application.

The principles of conditioning have been applied to a broad range of real-world behaviours and problems.

Token economy systems reward appropriate behaviour with tokens that are exchanged for privileges (operant conditioning). Successfully used in prisons and psychiatric wards.

Treatments like these are suitable for patients who lack 'insight' into their condition and are not capable of talking about their problems.

A limitation is the behaviourist approach portrays a mechanistic view.

Animals and humans are seen as passive and machine-like responders to the environment, with little conscious insight into their behaviour.

Other approaches, such as **social learning theory** and the **cognitive approach**, have placed much more emphasis on the mental events that occur during learning.

The processes that mediate between stimulus and response suggest that humans play a much more active role in their own learning.

A limitation is behaviourism is a form of environmental determinism.

The approach sees all behaviour as determined by past experiences that have been conditioned and ignores any influence that **free will** may have on behaviour.

Skinner suggested that free will was an illusion. When something happens we impose a sense of having made the decision but our past conditioning determined the outcome.

This is an extreme position and ignores the influence of conscious decision-making processes on behaviour (as suggested by the cognitive approach).

A limitation is that animal research has ethical and practical issues.

Although experimental procedures such as the Skinner box allowed behaviourists to maintain a high degree of control over their research subjects, critics have drawn attention to the ethical issues involved.

The animals involved were exposed to stressful and aversive conditions and this may have affected how they reacted to the experimental situation.

This means the **validity** of the findings from these studies might be questioned because the observed behaviour was not 'normal'.

CRAIG SWANSON © WWW. PERSPICUITY.COM

A former participant in the Skinner box studies struggles to find work.

KNOWLEDGE CHECK

1. Explain **two** assumptions of the behaviourist approach.
   (3 marks)
2. Outline Skinner's research into operant conditioning.
   (3 marks)
3. Explain how **two** types of reinforcement could be used by a parent to encourage their child to come home by 9pm on a school night.
   (4 marks)
4. Describe and evaluate the behaviourist approach in psychology. Refer to both Pavlov's and Skinner's research in your answer.
   (12 marks AS, 16 marks AL)

The learning approach: Social learning theory

Spec spotlight

Learning approaches: Social learning theory including imitation, identification, modelling, vicarious reinforcement, the role of meditational processes and Bandura's research.

Imitation – the sincerest form of flattery apparently

Barney is an eight-year-old boy. Although he has never been bullied at his primary school, several times he has seen an older boy bullying other children. He is physically aggressive, sometimes to get money or sweets, or just to show everyone who's boss.

Explain the social learning processes which may lead to Barney becoming a bully himself. Refer in your explanation to the roles of imitation, identification, modelling and vicarious reinforcement.

In terms of mediational processes, explain **three** ways in which Barney is unlikely to become a bully.

Note that modelling is a named term on the specification that can be used in two subtly different ways. From the observer's perspective, 'modelling' is imitating the behaviour of a role model. From the role model's perspective, it is demonstrating behaviour that may be imitated.

Key assumptions of social learning theory (SLT)

Learning that occurs *indirectly*.	Albert Bandura agreed with the **behaviourist approach** that learning occurs through experience. However, he also proposed that learning takes place in a social context through *observation* and *imitation* of others' behaviour.
Learning related to consequences of behaviour – *vicarious reinforcement*.	Children (and adults) observe other people's behaviour and take note of its consequences. Behaviour that is seen to be rewarded (reinforced) is much more likely to be copied than behaviour that is punished. Bandura called this vicarious reinforcement.
Mediational (cognitive) processes play a crucial role in learning.	There are four mediational processes in learning: 1. *Attention* – whether behaviour is noticed. 2. *Retention* – whether behaviour is remembered. 3. *Motor reproduction* – being able to do it. 4. *Motivation* – the will to perform the behaviour. The first two relate to the learning of behaviour, the last two to the performance of behaviour (so, unlike behaviourism, learning and performance do not have to occur together).
Identification with role models is important.	Children are more likely to imitate the behaviour of people with whom they identify. Such role models are similar to the observer, tend to be attractive and have high status.

Imitation of aggression Bandura's research	**Bandura's research 1** – children watched either: • An adult behaving aggressively towards a Bobo doll. • An adult behaving non-aggressively towards a Bobo doll. When given their own doll to play with, the children who had seen aggression were much more aggressive towards the doll.	**Bandura's research 2** – children saw adult who was: • Rewarded. • Punished. • There was no consequence. When given their own doll, the children who saw the aggression rewarded were much more aggressive themselves.

Children *model* aggressive behaviour	The Bobo doll studies suggest that children are likely to imitate (model) acts of violence if they observe these in an adult role model. It is also the case that **modelling** aggressive behaviour is more likely if such behaviour is seen to be rewarded (vicarious reinforcement).	

A strength is SLT emphasises the importance of cognitive factors in learning.

Neither **classical conditioning** nor **operant conditioning** can offer a comprehensive account of human learning on their own because cognitive factors are omitted.

Humans and animals store information about the behaviour of others and use this to make judgements about when it is appropriate to perform certain actions.

SLT provides a more complete explanation of human learning than the behaviourist approach by recognising the role of mediational processes.

A limitation is SLT relies too heavily on evidence from controlled lab studies.

Many of Bandura's ideas were developed through observation of children's behaviour in lab settings and this raises the problem of **demand characteristics**.

The main purpose of a Bobo doll is to hit it. So the children in those studies may have been behaving as they thought was expected.

Thus the research may tell us little about how children actually learn aggression in everyday life.

A limitation is SLT underestimates the influence of biological factors.

A consistent finding in the Bobo doll experiments was that boys showed more aggression than girls regardless of the specifics of the **experimental condition**.

This may be explained by differences in the levels of **testosterone**, which is present in greater quantities in boys and is linked to aggression.

This means that Bandura may have underplayed the important influence of biological factors on social learning.

A strength is SLT can account for cultural differences in behaviour.

Social learning principles can account for how children learn from other people around them, as well as through the media, and this can explain how cultural norms are transmitted.

This has proved useful in understanding a range of behaviours such as how children come to understand their gender role by imitating role models.

In contrast, the **biological approach** can only explain universal behaviours because human biological processes do not change with culture.

A strength is SLT is less determinist than the behaviourist approach.

Bandura emphasised *reciprocal determinism* – we are influenced by our environment, but we also exert an influence upon it through the behaviours we choose to perform.

This element of choice suggests that there is some **free will** in the way we behave.

This is a more realistic and flexible position than is suggested by the behaviourist approach as it recognises the role we play in shaping our own environment.

REVISION BOOSTER

Evaluation points like these do not just come in handy for longer essay-style questions. It is possible you might be asked for a single strength or limitation as part of a short answer question. Also, some questions ask for a 'brief discussion' of particular approaches. For such questions, two or three of these points would do the job nicely.

The word 'bobo' is Spanish for 'clown'. The word 'doll' is English for 'doll'.

The specification includes the terms: imitation, identification, modelling, vicarious reinforcement, the role of meditational processes and Bandura's research.

This means that exam questions may include any of these.

KNOWLEDGE CHECK

1. Using an example, explain what is meant by 'identification' in social learning theory. *(3 marks)*
2. Outline Bandura's research into social learning. *(3 marks)*
3. With reference to mediational processes in social learning, explain how a child might learn to bake a cake by watching his mother. *(6 marks)*
4. Describe and evaluate the social learning approach in psychology.
(12 marks AS, 16 marks AL)

The cognitive approach

Spec spotlight

The cognitive approach: the study of internal mental processes, the role of schema, the use of theoretical and computer models to explain and make inferences about mental processes.
The emergence of cognitive neuroscience.

REVISION BOOSTER

Note the difference between a theoretical model and a computer model. Both are named on the specification so you need to be able to provide an explanation and an example of each.

Also note the other terms that you can be examined on: internal mental processes, schema, inferences and the emergence of cognitive neuroscience.

PARIS
IN THE
THE SPRING

Did you spot the second 'the'? If not, that'll be your schema then.

Key assumptions of the cognitive approach

The scientific study of mental processes.	In direct contrast to the **behaviourist approach**, the cognitive approach argues that mental processes should be studied, e.g. studying perception and memory.
The role of *inference* in the study of mental processes.	Mental processes are 'private' and cannot be observed, so cognitive psychologists study them indirectly by making inferences (assumptions) about what is going on inside people's heads on the basis of their behaviour.
The use of *theoretical models* when describing and explaining mental processes.	The information processing approach suggests that information flows through a sequence of stages that include input, storage and retrieval, as in the *multi-store model* (see page 32).
The use of *computer models* when describing and explaining mental processes.	The 'computer analogy' suggests similarities in how computers and human minds process information. For instance, the use of a central processor (the brain), changing of information into a useable code and the use of 'stores' to hold information.
The idea of *schema* is central to the cognitive approach.	• Schema are packages of information developed through experience. • They act as a 'mental framework' for the interpretation of incoming information received by the cognitive system. • Babies are born with simple motor schema for innate behaviours such as sucking and grasping. • As we get older, our schema become more detailed and sophisticated.
The emergence of *cognitive neuroscience*.	• Cognitive neuroscience is the scientific study of the influence of brain structures (neuro) on mental processes (cognition). • With advances in brain scanning technology in the last twenty years, scientists have been able to describe the neurological basis of mental processing. • This includes research in memory that has linked *episodic* and *semantic memories* to opposite sides of the **prefrontal cortex** in the brain. • Scanning techniques have also proved useful in establishing the neurological basis of some disorders, e.g. the *parahippocampal gyrus* and OCD.

A strength is that the cognitive approach uses scientific and objective methods.

Cognitive psychologists have always employed controlled and rigorous methods of study, e.g. lab studies, in order to infer cognitive processes at work.

This has enabled the two fields of biology and cognitive psychology to come together (cognitive neuroscience).

This means that the study of the mind has established a credible, scientific basis.

A limitation is that the approach is based on machine reductionism.

Although there are similarities between the operations of the human mind and a computer (inputs and outputs, central processor, storage systems), the computer analogy has been criticised.

For instance, human emotion and motivation have been shown to influence accuracy of recall, e.g. in eyewitness accounts. These factors are not considered within the computer analogy.

Therefore, the cognitive approach oversimplifies human cognitive processing and ignores important aspects that influence performance.

Probably why they call it 'cog psychology'.

The approach is based on research that lacks external validity.

Cognitive psychologists are only able to infer mental processes from the behaviour they observe, so the approach sometimes suffers from being too abstract and theoretical.

Also, research is often carried out using artificial stimuli, such as recall of word lists in studies of memory which may not represent everyday experience.

Therefore, research into cognitive processes may lack external validity.

Apply it

Amber is two years old. Her parents have noticed that her play behaviour is not random, but seems to demonstrate certain patterns. For example, she is obsessed with Russian dolls and loves to get adults to remove each doll one at a time, then replace them over and over again. She really enjoys putting smaller objects inside larger ones and making dens and sitting in them.

Explain how the concept of a schema can help us understand such patterns of play.

A strength of the approach is the application to everyday life.

The cognitive approach is dominant in psychology today and has been applied to a wide range of practical and theoretical contexts.

For instance, the approach has made an important contribution to the field of *artificial intelligence* (AI) and the development of robots.

These exciting advances are likely to revolutionise how we live in the future.

KNOWLEDGE CHECK

1. Using an example, outline what cognitive psychologists mean by the word 'schema'. *(3 marks)*
2. Briefly explain how theoretical models are used in cognitive psychology to make inferences about mental processes. *(4 marks)*
3. Outline the emergence of cognitive neuroscience in psychology. *(6 marks)*
4. Briefly discuss the cognitive approach. *(8 marks)*
5. Describe and evaluate the cognitive approach in psychology. *(12 marks AS, 16 marks AL)*

A strength is that the approach is less determinist than other approaches.

The cognitive approach is based on **soft determinism**, recognising that our cognitive system can only operate within certain limits, but that we are free to think before responding to a stimulus.

This is in contrast to the **behaviourist approach** which suggests that we are passive 'slaves' to the environment and lack free choice in our behaviour.

The cognitive approach takes a more reasonable and flexible middle-ground position in the **free will**-determinism debate and is more in line with our subjective sense of free will.

The biological approach

Spec spotlight

The biological approach: the influence of genes, biological structures and neurochemistry on behaviour. Genotype and phenotype, genetic basis of behaviour, evolution and behaviour.

Yeah they look cute now but wait until they wake up.

Wilson's disease is a rare genetic disorder which can affect several of the body's systems, including the brain. This results in symptoms such as clumsiness, speech problems, difficulty in concentrating, depression and anxiety. It is caused by the body storing too much copper, a mineral which we need in just tiny amounts. There is no cure. But the disorder can be managed by reducing the amount of copper in the diet, and carefully monitoring blood and urine, so the individual can develop normally.

Using Wilson's disease as an example, explain the difference between genotype and phenotype.

Key assumptions of the biological approach

Everything psychological is at first biological.	If we want to fully understand human behaviour we must look to biological structures and processes within the body, such as *genes*, *neurochemistry* and the *nervous system*.
Behaviour has a *genetic* and *neurochemical* basis.	Behaviours are inherited in the same way as physical characteristics such as height or eye colour. For example, the 5HT1-D beta gene implicated in OCD.
	Neurochemistry also explains behaviour, for example low levels of **serotonin** in OCD.
The mind and body are one and the same.	From a biological perspective, the mind lives in the brain – meaning that all thoughts, feelings and behaviour ultimately have a physical basis.
	This is in contrast to the **cognitive approach** which sees the mind as separate from the brain.
Twin studies are used to investigate the genetic basis of behaviour.	*Concordance rates* between twins are calculated – the extent to which twins share the same characteristic.
	Higher concordance rates among identical (monozygotic, MZ) twins than non-identical (dizygotic, DZ) twins is evidence of a genetic basis. For example, 68% of MZ twins both have OCD compared with 31% of DZ twins (Nestadt *et al.* 2010).
The difference between *genotype* and *phenotype*.	• A person's genotype is their actual genetic make-up.
	• Phenotype is the way that genes are expressed through physical, behavioural and psychological characteristics.
	• The expression of genotype (phenotype) is influenced by environmental factors.
	• For example, *phenylketonuria (PKU)* is a genetic disorder that can be prevented by a restricted diet.
	• This suggests that much of human behaviour depends on the interaction of nature and nurture.
The *theory of evolution* is used by the biological approach to explain many aspects of behaviour.	• Charles Darwin (1859) proposed the theory of natural selection.
	• Any genetically determined behaviour that enhances survival *and* reproduction will be passed on to future generations.
	• Such genes are described as adaptive and give the possessor and their offspring advantages.
	• For instance, attachment behaviours in newborns promote survival and are therefore adaptive and naturally selected.

A strength of the approach is its use of scientific methods of investigation.

In order to investigate the genetic and biological basis of behaviour, the biological approach makes use of a range of precise and highly scientific methods.

These include scanning techniques (e.g. **fMRIs**) and drug trials. It is possible to accurately measure biological and neural processes in ways that are not open to bias.

This means that the biological approach is based on reliable data.

The biological approach has real-life application.

Increased understanding of biochemical processes in the brain has led to the development of psychoactive drugs that treat serious mental disorders, such as depression.

Although these drugs are not effective for all patients, they have revolutionised treatment for many.

This is a strength of the approach because it means that sufferers are able to live a relatively normal life, rather than in hospital.

Biology is the only science in which multiplication is the same thing as division.

Causal conclusions about neurotransmitters are difficult to establish.

The role of neurotransmitters in mental illness comes from studies that show a particular drug reduces symptoms of the disorder by changing levels of neurotransmitter. It is assumed that the neurotransmitter is the cause.

This is a bit like assuming that the cause of a headache is lack of paracetamol simply because paracetamol is effective in relieving symptoms of a headache.

This is a limitation because the biological approach is claiming to have discovered causes where only an association exists.

Apply it

Biological psychologists believe that behaviours have evolved because they provide some advantage, in terms of allowing us to adapt to our environments. Examples from this book include: (1) conforming to the behaviour of other members of a group; (2) having both long-term and short-term memories; (3) suffering from depression (which many psychologists believe has a genetic basis).

For each of these examples, explain what the adaptive advantages could be.

A limitation is that the approach is based on a determinist view of behaviour.

The biological approach is determinist in that it sees human behaviour as governed by internal, biological causes over which we have no control.

However, this is at odds with the legal system which sees offenders as responsible for their actions. The discovery of a 'criminal gene' may complicate this principle.

Such research may have (possibly negative) implications for wider society as criminals may be able to excuse their behaviour.

KNOWLEDGE CHECK

1. Outline **two** key features of the biological approach in psychology. (6 marks)

2. Using an example, distinguish between 'genotype' and 'phenotype'. (3 marks)

3. Explain what is meant by 'evolution and behaviour'. Illustrate your answer with an example of a human or non-human behaviour. (3 marks)

4. Describe and evaluate the biological approach in psychology.
(12 marks AS, 16 marks AL)

A methodological problem is the difficulty of separating nature and nurture.

Identical twins, non-identical twins and members of the same family all have genetic similarities, so any similarity in the way they behave must be genetic from a biological perspective.

However, the fact that family members are exposed to similar environmental conditions is an important **confounding variable**.

This is a problem for the biological approach because findings could be just as easily interpreted as supporting nurture rather than nature.

Biopsychology: The nervous system

Spec spotlight

Biopsychology

The divisions of the nervous system: central and peripheral (somatic and autonomic).

The function of the endocrine system: glands and hormones.

The fight or flight response and the role of adrenaline.

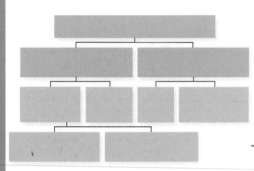

You might have to label a diagram in the exam. Nervous..?

Apply it

Leah is being interviewed for a job. It's really important to her and everything is going fine, until one interviewer asks her a question and she suddenly realises she doesn't know the answer. She tries hard to remember the information she needs but can't concentrate. She can hear her heart beating faster, her face is reddening, her hands are shaking and she feels sick.

Explain the roles of (1) the CNS, (2) the ANS, and (3) the endocrine system in Leah's behaviour.

The nervous system

The key features of the *nervous system*.	The nervous system is a specialised network of cells and our primary communication system. It has two main functions: 1. To collect, process and respond to information in the environment; 2. To co-ordinate the working of different organs and cells in the body. It is divided into the central nervous system and the peripheral nervous system.
The structure and function of the *central nervous system* (CNS)	• The CNS is made up of the brain and the spinal cord. • The brain is the centre of all conscious awareness. • The outer layer of the brain, the cerebral cortex, is highly developed in humans and is what distinguishes our higher mental functions from those of animals. • The spinal cord is an extension of the brain and is responsible for reflex actions. • It passes messages to and from the brain and connects nerves to the PNS.
The structure and function of the *peripheral nervous system* (PNS)	• The PNS transmits messages, via millions of neurons, to and from the nervous system. • The PNS is further sub-divided into the *autonomic nervous system* (ANS) and the *somatic nervous system* (SNS). • The ANS governs vital functions in the body such as breathing, heart rate, digestion, sexual arousal and stress responses. • The SNS controls muscle movement and receives information from sensory receptors.

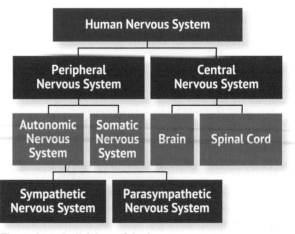

The major sub-divisions of the human nervous system.

The endocrine system

The key features of the *endocrine system*.	The endocrine system works alongside the nervous system to control vital functions in the body through the action of hormones.
	It works much more slowly than the nervous system but has widespread and powerful effects.

© Mike Baldwin / Cornered

Glands	Glands are organs in the body that produce hormones.
	The major endocrine gland is the *pituitary gland*, located in the brain. It is called the 'master gland' because it controls the release of hormones from all the other endocrine glands in the body.

Hormones	Hormones are secreted in the bloodstream and affect any cell in the body that has a receptor for that particular hormone.
	For example, *thyroxine* produced by the thyroid gland affects cells in the heart and also cells throughout the body which increase metabolic rates. This in turn affects growth rates.

REVISION BOOSTER

Questions in this section are likely to be either descriptive or application. There is very little scope for evaluation/discussion in this section so an essay – at AS at least – in biopsychology is very unlikely.

The endocrine system and the ANS work together. For example, the *fight or flight response*.	Often the endocrine system and the ANS work in parallel, for instance during a *stressful event*. • When a stressor is perceived, the *hypothalamus* triggers activity in the *sympathetic branch* of the ANS. The ANS changes from its normal resting state (the *parasympathetic state*) to the physiologically aroused sympathetic state. • The stress hormone *adrenaline* is released from the *adrenal medulla* into the bloodstream. • Adrenaline triggers physiological changes in target organs in the body and causes, e.g. increased heart rate, dilation of the pupils, decreased production of saliva. This is called the fight or flight response. • Once the threat has passed, the parasympathetic nervous system returns the body to its resting state. This acts as a 'brake' and reduces the activities of the body that were increased by the actions of the sympathetic branch (sometimes referred to as the 'rest and digest' response).

Sympathetic state	Parasympathetic state
Increases heart rate	Decreases heart rate
Increases breathing rate	Decreases breathing rate
Dilates pupils	Constricts pupils
Inhibits digestion	Stimulates digestion
Inhibits saliva production	Stimulates saliva production
Contracts rectum	Relaxes rectum

KNOWLEDGE CHECK

1. Using an example, explain what is meant by the 'fight or flight response'. *(4 marks)*
2. Identify and outline **two** divisions of the peripheral nervous system *(4 marks)*
3. Identify and describe **two** glands of the endocrine system. *(4 marks)*
4. Explain the difference between the nervous system and the endocrine system. *(3 marks)*

Biopsychology: Neurons

Spec spotlight

Biopsychology

The structure and function of sensory, relay and motor neurons.

The process of synaptic transmission including reference to neurotransmitters, excitation and inhibition.

REVISION BOOSTER

It is important that you can describe the structure and function of each of the three types of neuron as these are specifically named on the spec.

cell body — sensory neuron

direction of conduction

nodes of Ranvier

myelin sheath

relay neuron

axon

cell body

dendrites — axon

motor neuron

Yeah, my heart stood still, a neuron ron yeah a neuron ron.

Ask your parents...

The structure and function of neurons

Types and function of *neurons*.

There are 100 billion nerve cells (neurons) in the human nervous system, 80% of which are located in the brain.

By transmitting signals *electrically* and *chemically*, these provide the nervous system with its primary means of communication.

There are three types of neuron:

1. *Motor neurons* connect the CNS to effectors such as muscles and glands. They have short dendrites and long axons.

2. *Sensory neurons* carry messages from the PNS to the CNS. They have long dendrites and short axons.

3. *Relay neurons* connect sensory neurons to motor or other relay neurons. They have short dendrites and short axons.

The structure of a neuron.

Neurons vary in size but all share the same basic structure:

- *Cell body* (or soma) – includes a nucleus which contains the genetic material of the cell.

- *Dendrites* – branch-like structures that protrude from the cell body. These carry nerve impulses from neighbouring neurons towards the cell body.

- *Axon* – carries the electrical impulse away from the cell body down the length of the neuron.

   ○ It is covered in a fatty layer of *myelin sheath* that protects the axon.

   ○ Gaps in the axon called *nodes of Ranvier* speed up the transmission of the impulse.

- *Terminal buttons* at the end of the axon communicate with the next neuron in the chain across a gap called the *synapse*.

Electric transmission.

The firing of a neuron.

When a neuron is in a resting state the inside of the cell is *negatively charged* compared to the outside.

When a neuron is activated, the inside of the cell becomes *positively charged* for a split second causing an *action potential* to occur.

This creates an electrical impulse that travels down the axon towards the end of the neuron.

Synaptic transmission

A *synapse*	Each neuron is separated from the next by a tiny gap called the synapse.

Synapse

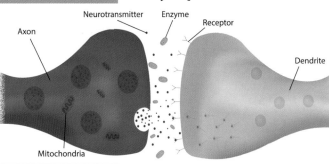

My friend just burst into my room and asked me what an electrical synapse in the human body was.

The nerve.

Chemical transmission. The events that occur at the synapse.	Signals within neurons are transmitted electrically; however, signals between neurons are transmitted chemically across the synapse. When the electrical impulse reaches the end of the neuron (the *presynaptic terminal*) it triggers the release of *neurotransmitter* from tiny sacs called *synaptic vesicles*. Once the neurotransmitter crosses the gap, it is taken up by the *postsynaptic receptor* site on the next neuron. The chemical message is converted back into an electrical impulse and the process of electric transmission begins.
Neurotransmitters.	Neurotransmitters are chemicals that diffuse across the synapse to the next neuron in the chain. Several dozen neurotransmitters have been identified. Each has its own specific molecular structure that fits perfectly into a post-synaptic receptor site, like a lock and key. Each has specific functions. For example: • *Acetylcholine* (ACh) found where a motor neuron meets a muscle, causing muscles to contract. • **Serotonin** affects mood and social behaviour (among other things) which is why it has been implicated as a cause of depression.
Excitation and inhibition.	Neurotransmitters generally have either an excitatory or inhibitory effect on the neighbouring neuron. • *Adrenaline* – generally excitatory, increasing the positive charge of the postsynaptic neuron, making it more likely the neuron will fire. • *Serotonin* – generally inhibitory, increasing the negative charge of the postsynaptic neuron, making it less likely the neuron will fire. • **Dopamine** is an unusual neurotransmitter as it is equally likely to have excitatory or inhibitory effects on the next neuron in the chain.

Apply it

Sabiha loves chocolate. She eats it all the time and really believes that it gives her a 'boost' and makes her feel happier. Her friend Bev tells her that's probably because chocolate contains chemicals that have a real effect on the neurotransmitters of the nervous system.

Use your knowledge of synaptic transmission to explain what is happening at Sabiha's synapses.

KNOWLEDGE CHECK

1. Explain the difference between a motor neuron and a relay neuron. *(2 marks)*
2. Briefly describe the structure of a neuron. *(3 marks)*
3. With reference to neurotransmitters, explain what is meant by excitation and inhibition. *(4 marks)*
4. Briefly explain the sequence of events that take place at the synapse. *(4 marks)*

The psychodynamic approach   A LEVEL ONLY

Spec spotlight

The psychodynamic approach: the role of the unconscious, the structure of personality, that is Id, Ego and Superego, defence mechanisms including repression, denial and displacement, psychosexual stages.

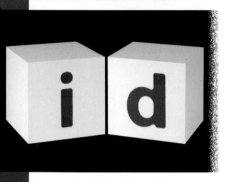

Id. A handy word to know if you're running out of tiles in Scrabble.

REVISION BOOSTER

The psychodynamic approach is complex and wide-ranging. It would be easy to overdo the AO1 content in an essay on this approach. Keep description of things like Freud's psychosexual stages to a minimum and only select a few examples.

Apply it

Gregory got his girlfriend's and his mum's names mixed up the other day. Felix is only interested in satisfying his own desires. Lisbeth feels guilty all the time over the smallest things. Heathcliffe's parents are having trouble getting him potty-trained. Alanis is five and wants to marry her daddy when she grows up. There are holes in Donald's bedroom door where he punches it when he comes in from work.

Identify the psychodynamic concepts on this page that could apply to these people. Explain your choices.

Key assumptions of the psychodynamic approach

The *unconscious mind* has an important influence on behaviour.	Sigmund Freud suggested the mind is made up of: • Conscious – what we are aware of. • Pre-conscious – thoughts we may become aware of through dreams and 'slips of the tongue'. • Unconscious – a vast storehouse of biological drives and instincts that influence our behaviour.
Tripartite structure of personality. Dynamic interaction between the three parts determines behaviour.	Freud saw personality as having three parts: • *Id* – primitive part of the personality operates on the *pleasure principle*, demands instant gratification. • *Ego* – works on the *reality principle* and is the mediator between the id and superego. • *Superego* – internalised sense of right and wrong, based on *morality principle*. Punishes the ego through guilt.
Five *psychosexual stages* that determine adult personality.	Each stage is marked by a different conflict that the child must resolve to move on to the next. Any conflict that is unresolved leads to fixation where the child becomes 'stuck' and carries behaviours associated with that stage through to adult life.
The sequence of stages is fixed.	Oral (0–1 years) – pleasure focus = mouth, the mother's breast is the object of desire. Anal (1–3 years) – pleasure focus = anus, the child gains pleasure from withholding and eliminating faeces. Phallic (3–5 years) – pleasure focus = genital area. Latency – earlier conflicts are repressed. Genital (puberty) – sexual desires become conscious.
The *Oedipus complex* is an important psychosexual conflict occurring at the phallic stage.	In the phallic stage, little boys develop incestuous feelings towards their mother and a murderous hatred for their father. Later boys repress their feelings for their mother and identify with their father, taking on his gender role and moral values. Girls of the same age experience penis envy.
Defence mechanisms are used by the ego to keep the id 'in check' and reduce anxiety.	Unconscious strategies used by the ego, for example: • *Repression* – forcing a distressing memory out of the conscious mind. • *Denial* – refusing to acknowledge reality. • *Displacement* – transferring feelings from their true source onto a substitute target.

A strength is that the psychodynamic approach has explanatory power.

Although Freud's theory is controversial and often bizarre it has had huge influence on Western contemporary thought.

It has been used to explain a wide range of behaviours (moral, mental disorders) and drew attention to the influence of childhood on adult personality.

Alongside **behaviourism**, it was the dominant approach in psychology for the first half of the twentieth century.

The case study method that Freud relied on has been criticised.

Freud's ideas were developed using a small number of case studies, e.g. Little Hans, Dora and the Rat Man. Critics have suggested that it is not possible to make universal claims about human nature based on such a limited sample.

Although Freud's observations were detailed and carefully recorded, his interpretations were highly subjective and it is unlikely that any other researcher would have drawn the same conclusions.

In comparison with other approaches, Freud's methods lacked scientific rigour.

The psychodynamic approach includes lots of untestable concepts.

Karl Popper (philosopher of science) argued that the psychodynamic approach does not meet the scientific criterion of *falsification*, in the sense that it cannot be proved or disproved.

Many of Freud's concepts, such as the Id or the Oedipus complex, occur at an unconscious level making them difficult, if not impossible, to test.

This affords psychodynamic theory the status of pseudoscience ('fake' science) rather than real science.

Freudian slip joke: Sigmund Freud walked into a bra...

A strength is that the approach has practical application in the real world.

Freud introduced a new form of therapy: *psychoanalysis*. The therapy is designed to access the unconscious mind using a range of techniques such as hypnosis and dream analysis.

Psychoanalysis is most suitable for individuals suffering from mild neuroses but has been criticised as inappropriate for people with severe mental disorders such as schizophrenia.

That said, psychoanalysis is the forerunner to many modern-day psychotherapies and 'talking cures' that have since been established.

KNOWLEDGE CHECK

1. The psychodynamic approach places emphasis on the role of unconscious in behaviour. Using an example, explain the role of the unconscious in behaviour.   *(4 marks)*

2. Explain how **one** defence mechanism might help someone cope with the anxiety of losing their job.
          (3 marks)

3. Name and explain **one** of Freud's psychosexual stages of development.   *(3 marks)*.

4. Describe and evaluate the psychodynamic approach in psychology.
     (12 marks AS, 16 marks AL)

A limitation of the approach is that it is based on psychic determinism.

The psychodynamic approach explains all behaviour as determined by unconscious conflicts that are rooted in childhood.

Even something as apparently random as a 'slip of the tongue' is driven by unconscious forces and has deep symbolic meaning.

This is an extreme determinist stance and suggests that **free will** may have no influence on behaviour.

The humanistic approach   A LEVEL ONLY

Spec spotlight

Humanistic psychology: free will, self-actualisation and Maslow's hierarchy of needs, focus on the self, congruence, the role of conditions of worth. The influence of counselling psychology.

Humanistic psychologists believe we have 'free will' – a philosophical position which suggests we are able to reject internal and external influences. Not to be confused with 'Free Willy', which is a film about a whale.

Apply it

Anika feels depressed because she feels that her life is empty and worthless. There were so many things she wanted to do and be but now sees that it's too late. She sees a person-centred therapist for counselling.

Referring to both Maslow's hierarchy of needs and Rogers' concept of congruence, explain how Anika could be helped to recover from depression.

Key assumptions of the humanistic approach

The concept of **free will** is central.	Humanistic psychologists reject attempts to establish scientific principles of human behaviour.
	We are all unique, and psychology should concern itself with the study of subjective experience rather than general laws – a person-centred approach.
Maslow's *hierarchy of needs* has *self-actualisation* at the top.	Self-actualisation refers to the innate tendency that each of us has to want to achieve our full potential and become the best we can possibly be.
	In Abraham Maslow's hierarchy of needs the four lower levels (deficiency needs) must be met before the individual can work towards self-actualisation – a growth need.
Focus on the self.	The self refers to the ideas and values that characterise 'I' and 'me' and includes perception of 'what I am' and 'what I can do'.
The aim of therapy is to establish *congruence* between the self-concept and the ideal self.	Carl Rogers argued that personal growth requires an individual's concept of self to be congruent with their ideal self (the person they want to be).
	If too big a gap, the person will experience a state of incongruence and self-actualisation isn't possible.
Parents who impose *conditions of worth* may prevent personal growth.	Issues such as worthlessness and low self-esteem have their roots in childhood and are due to a lack of *unconditional positive regard* from our parents.
	A parent who sets boundaries on their love for their child (conditions of worth) by claiming 'I will only love you if...' is storing up psychological problems for that child in future.
The humanistic approach has had a lasting influence on *counselling psychology*.	In Rogers' client-centred therapy an effective therapist should provide the client with three things:

In Rogers' client-centred therapy an effective therapist should provide the client with three things:

- Genuineness
- Empathy
- Unconditional positive regard

The aim is to increase feelings of self-worth and reduce incongruence between the self-concept and the ideal self.

Rogers work transformed psychotherapy. 'Non-directive' counselling techniques are practised, not only in clinical settings, but throughout education, health, social work and industry.

Humanistic psychology is anti-reductionist which may make it more meaningful.

Humanistic psychologists reject any attempt to break up behaviour and experience into smaller components.

They advocate **holism** – the idea that subjective experience can only be understood by considering the whole person (their relationships, past, present and future, etc.).

This approach may have more **validity** than its alternatives by considering meaningful human behaviour within its real-life context.

The approach has limited application in the real world.

It is true that Rogerian therapy has revolutionised counselling techniques and Maslow's hierarchy of needs has been used to explain motivation, particularly in the workplace.

However, compared to other approaches, humanistic psychology has had limited impact within psychology as a whole – perhaps because it lacks a sound evidence base.

As a result, the approach has been described, not as a comprehensive theory, but as a rather loose set of abstract concepts.

A strength is the approach portrays a positive image of the human condition.

Humanistic psychologists have been praised for promoting a positive image of the human condition – seeing people as in control of their lives and having the freedom to change.

Freud saw human beings as slaves to their past and claimed all of us existed somewhere between 'common unhappiness and absolute despair'.

Humanistic psychology offers a refreshing and optimistic alternative.

A limitation is that the approach includes untestable concepts.

Humanistic psychology includes a number of vague ideas that are abstract and difficult to test, such as 'self-actualisation' and 'congruence'.

Rogers did attempt to introduce more rigour into his work by developing the *Q-sort* – an objective measure of progress in therapy.

As would be expected of an approach that is 'anti-scientific', humanistic psychology is short on empirical evidence.

A limitation is that the approach may be guilty of a Western cultural bias.

Many of the ideas that are central to humanistic psychology, such as individual freedom, autonomy and personal growth, would be more readily associated with **individualist** cultures in the Western world such as the United States.

Collectivist cultures such as India, which emphasise the needs of the group and interdependence, may not identify so easily with the ideals and values of humanistic psychology.

Therefore, it is possible that the approach would not travel well and is a product of the cultural context within which it was developed.

Ella Fitzgerald famously said, 'It isn't where you've come from, it's where you're going that counts'. Unlike psychoanalysis, Rogerian therapy looks forward not back.

KNOWLEDGE CHECK

1. Explain what humanistic psychologists mean by 'conditions of worth'. Give an example. *(3 marks)*
2. Outline and briefly discuss the humanistic concept of self-actualisation. *(4 marks)*
3. Briefly evaluate humanistic psychology. *(6 marks)*
4. Describe and evaluate the humanistic approach in psychology. *(12 marks AS, 16 marks AL)*

Comparison of approaches   A LEVEL ONLY

Spec spotlight

Comparison of approaches.

Comparing apples is somewhat easier than comparing psychological approaches....

REVISION BOOSTER

The phrase 'comparison of approaches' is one that only appears on the A Level specification, not the AS. This means you cannot be explicitly asked to do this on the AS exam paper.

Having said that, comparing approaches is a good way of getting AO3 evaluation marks in an essay – as long as you make it clear how the comparison highlights a strength or limitation of the approach you have been asked about.

Apply it

This spread presents several important issues in psychology. The various approaches have unique perspectives on each one, for example nature versus nurture.

Which approach do you think most emphasises nature, and which most emphasises nurture? Explain how they differ.

Now choose **two** approaches which take a similar line on this issue (i.e. both nature or both nurture). How are they similar?

(You could answer the same questions for the other issues, such as determinism and reductionism.)

Approach	Behaviourist	Social learning	Cognitive
Views on development	The processes that underpin learning are continuous, occurring at any age.	Same as behaviourism.	Stage theories of child development, particularly the idea of concept formation (schema) as child gets older.
Nature versus nurture	Babies are 'blank slates' at birth. All behaviour comes about through learned associations and reinforcements.	As for behaviourism with additional processes of observation and imitation.	Recognises that many of our information-processing abilities are innate, but are constantly refined by experience.
Reductionism	Reduces complex learning into stimulus-response units for ease of testing in a controlled lab environment.	Recognises how cognitive factors interact with the external environment.	Machine reductionism: use of the computer analogy and the fact that it ignores human emotion.
Determinism	All behaviour is environmentally determined by external forces that we cannot control.	We are influenced by our environment and also exert some influence upon it (*reciprocal determinism*).	Suggests we are the 'choosers' of our own behaviour, but only within the limits of what we know (**soft determinism**).
Explanation and treatment of abnormal/ atypical behaviour	Abnormality arises from maladaptive or faulty learning. Behavioural therapies take a symptom-based approach to the unlearning of behaviour.	Principles such as **modelling** have been used to explain the development of aggressive behaviour.	Led to cognitive therapies such as cognitive behaviour therapy (CBT) in the treatment of depression, which aims to eradicate faulty thinking.

Biological	Psychodynamic	Humanistic
Genetically determined maturational changes influence behaviour, e.g. cognitive/intellectual development.	The most coherent theory of development, tying concepts and processes to age-related stages.	The development of the self is ongoing throughout life.
'Anatomy is destiny': behaviour stems from the genetic blueprint we inherit from our parents.	Suggests that much of our behaviour is driven by biological drives and instincts, but also sees the child's relationships with its parents as crucial.	Regards parents, friends and wider society as having a critical impact on the person's self-concept.
Reduces and explains human behaviour at the level of the gene or neuron.	Reduces behaviour to the influence of biological drives and instincts, although also sees personality as a dynamic, **holistic** interaction.	Anti-reductionist, based on holistic investigation of all aspects of the individual.
A form of genetic determinism, much of our behaviour is directed by innate influences.	Unconscious forces drive our behaviour (psychic determinism) and these are rationalised by our conscious minds.	Human beings have **free will** and are active agents who determine their own development.
Psychoactive drugs that regulate chemical imbalances in the brain have revolutionised the treatment of mental disorders.	Anxiety disorders emerge from unconscious conflicts and overuse of defence mechanisms. Psychoanalysis aims to put people in touch with their unconscious thoughts.	Humanistic therapy, or counselling, is based on the idea that reducing incongruence will stimulate personal growth.

The TV usually does what we tell it to – but to what extent are we in control of our thoughts and behaviour?

Eclecticism

Worth noting that most modern psychologists would take an eclectic (multidisciplinary) approach to the study of human behaviour. Very few researchers work entirely within one approach.

Eclecticism refers to the combining of several approaches and/or methods to provide a more comprehensive account.

The **diathesis-stress model** suggests that many mental disorders are a complex interaction of genetic predisposition and environmental triggers.

Combining treatment options from several different perspectives, e.g. drugs, cognitive therapy, family therapy, has led to more effective outcomes for patients and lower relapse rates.

KNOWLEDGE CHECK

1. Outline **one** way in which the psychodynamic approach and humanistic psychology overlap. *(3 marks)*
2. Briefly discuss **one** difference between the social learning approach and the behaviourist approach. *(4 marks)*
3. Outline and briefly compare the biological approach and the cognitive approach. *(10 marks)*

Definitions of abnormality I

Spec spotlight

Definitions of abnormality: including statistical infrequency and deviation from social norms.

Statistical infrequency

Defining abnormality in terms of statistics.	The most obvious way to define anything as 'normal' or 'abnormal' is in terms of the number of times it is observed. *Statistics* is about analysing numbers.
Behaviour that is rarely seen is abnormal.	Any relatively 'usual', or often seen, behaviour can be thought of as 'normal'. Any behaviour that is different, or rare, is 'abnormal', i.e. a statistical infrequency.
Example: IQ and *intellectual disability disorder*.	IQ is *normally distributed* (see left). The average IQ is 100. Most people have an IQ between 85 and 115, only 2% have a score below 70. Those individuals scoring below 70 are statistically unusual or 'abnormal' and are diagnosed with intellectual disability disorder.

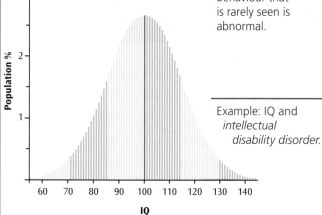

REVISION BOOSTER

Questions in the exam which require a description of a definition of abnormality may be worth *2 or 3 marks*. Therefore it makes sense to identify three key things you would say for each definition (as we have done here). In an exam, if you write these three things and explain each one, you would certainly get the full *3 marks*.

Abnormality can be defined as behaviour that is statistically infrequent or behaviour that doesn't fit with social norms.

Deviation from social norms

Abnormality is based on social context.	When a person behaves in a way that is different from how they are expected to behave they may be defined as abnormal. Societies and social groups make collective judgements about 'correct' behaviours in particular circumstances.
Three types of consequences of behaviour.	There are relatively few behaviours that would be considered universally abnormal therefore definitions are related to cultural context. This includes historical differences within the same society. For example, homosexuality is viewed as abnormal in some cultures but not others and was considered abnormal in our society in the past.
Example: *antisocial personality disorder* (APD).	One important symptom of antisocial personality disorder (formerly psychopathy) is a failure to conform to 'lawful and culturally normative ethical behaviour'. In other words, a psychopath is abnormal because they deviate from social norms or standards. They generally lack empathy.

A strength of statistical infrequency is its real-life application.

All assessment of patients with mental disorders includes some comparison to statistical norms.	Intellectual disability disorder demonstrates how statistical infrequency can be used.	Statistical infrequency is thus a useful part of clinical assessment.

A limitation is that unusual characteristics can also be positive.

If very few people display a behaviour, that makes the behaviour statistically abnormal but doesn't mean the person requires treatment.	IQ scores over 130 are just as unusual as those below 70, but not regarded as undesirable and requiring treatment.	This is a serious limitation of the concept of statistical infrequency and means it should never be used alone to make a diagnosis.

A further limitation is that not everyone unusual benefits from a label.

When someone is living a happy and fulfilled life, there is no benefit to them being labelled as abnormal.	Someone with a very low IQ who was not distressed or out of work, etc., would not need a diagnosis of intellectual disability.	Being labelled as abnormal might have a negative effect on the way others view them and the way they see themselves.

Deviation from social norms is not a sole explanation of abnormality.

Antisocial personality disorder (APD) shows there is a place for deviation from social norms in thinking about what is abnormal.	However, there are other factors to consider, e.g. distress to other people due to APD.	So in practice, deviation from social norms is never the sole reason for defining abnormality.

A limitation is that social norms are culturally relative.

A person from one cultural group may label someone from another group as abnormal using their standards rather than the person's standards.	For example, hearing voices is socially acceptable in some cultures but would be seen as a sign of abnormality in the UK.	This creates problems for people from one culture living within another cultural group.

A further limitation is that the definition could lead to human rights abuses.

Too much reliance on deviation from social norms to understand abnormality can lead to a systematic abuse of human rights.	Drapetomania (black slaves trying to escape) and nymphomania (women attracted to working-class men) are examples of how diagnosis was used for social control.	Such classifications appear ridiculous but some psychologists argue that some modern abnormal classifications are abuses of people's right to be different.

I've been described as an insomniac atheist dyslexic – I lay awake all night wondering if there is a Dog.

Gloria is a 12-year-old girl who has a very high IQ (in the top 1% of the population). But many people have commented on her poor social skills. She gets uncomfortably close to people in conversation, and makes hurtful and offensive comments (e.g. about appearance). She maintains eye contact for long periods, and appears to have no fear of strangers.

Using the statistical infrequency and deviation from social norms definitions, explain why Gloria could be considered abnormal.

Are there any reasons why Gloria should not be regarded as abnormal? Explain at least two of them.

REVISION BOOSTER

On the left we have identified FIVE evaluation points, and for each provided THREE levels of elaboration.

On page 6 we suggested there are two routes for doing evaluation in an AS essay (6 marks AO3) - either do THREE well-elaborated points or FIVE 'intermediate' evaluations.

KNOWLEDGE CHECK

1. Outline **two** definitions of abnormality. *(6 marks)*
2. Explain **one** criticism of statistical infrequency as a definition of abnormality. *(3 marks)*
3. Briefly evaluate the deviation from social norms definition of abnormality. *(4 marks)*
4. Outline and evaluate statistical infrequency and deviation from social norms as definitions of abnormality. *(12 marks AS, 16 marks AL)*

Definitions of abnormality II

Spec spotlight

Definitions of abnormality: including failure to function adequately and deviation from ideal mental health.

At a festival, most people will fail to maintain basic standards of nutrition and hygiene.

Stephen Gough is a former Royal Marine known as 'the Naked Rambler' because he spends most of his time walking across Britain wearing nothing more than socks, boots, a rucksack and a hat. He has been arrested more than 20 times and spent almost eight of the last nine years in prison. He has refused to wear clothes at many of his trials. Mr Gough is rational and lucid about his reasons for behaving like this. He does not go out of his way to offend people. He believes it is his human right to go where he likes without clothes.

In terms of failure to function adequately and deviation from ideal mental health, would you say that Stephen Gough should be considered abnormal? Explain your answer with reference to psychological concepts.

REVISION BOOSTER

Some students find it difficult to remember which definition is which – try to focus less on the word 'deviation' or 'failure' and more on 'statistical', 'social norms', 'function adequately' and 'mental health'.

Failure to function adequately

Inability to cope with everyday living.	A person may cross the line between normal and abnormal at the point that they cannot deal with the demands of everyday life – they fail to function adequately. For instance, not being able to hold down a job, maintain relationships or maintain basic standards of nutrition and hygiene.
Rosenhan and Seligman (1989) proposed signs of failure to cope.	When someone is not coping: • They no longer conform to interpersonal rules, e.g. maintaining personal space. • They experience personal distress. • They behave in a way that is irrational or dangerous.
Example: *intellectual disability disorder.*	Having a very low IQ is a statistical infrequency but diagnosis would not be made on this basis alone. There would have to be clear signs that, as a result of this, the person was not able to cope with the demands of everyday living. So intellectual disability disorder is an example of failure to function adequately.

Deviation from ideal mental health

Changing the emphasis.	A different way to look at normality and abnormality is to think about what makes someone 'normal' and psychologically healthy. Then identify anyone who deviates from this ideal.
Jahoda listed 8 criteria.	Marie Jahoda (1958) suggested the following criteria for ideal mental health: 1. We have no symptoms or distress. 2. We are rational and perceive ourselves accurately. 3. We self-actualise. 4. We can cope with stress. 5. We have a realistic view of the world. 6. We have good self-esteem and lack guilt. 7. We are independent of other people. 8. We can successfully work, love and enjoy our leisure.
Inevitable overlap between definitions.	Someone's inability to keep a job may be a sign of their failure to cope with the pressures of work (failure to function). Or as a deviation from the ideal of successfully working.

Failure to function adequately recognises the patient's perspective.

This may not be an entirely satisfactory approach because it is difficult to assess distress.

However, the definition acknowledges that the experience of the patient (and/or others) is important.

It captures the experience of many people who need help and is useful for assessing abnormality.

A limitation is that this is the same as deviation from social norms.

It can be hard to say when someone is really failing to function or just deviating from social norms.

People who live alternative lifestyles or do extreme sports could be seen as behaving maladaptively.

If we treat these behaviours as 'failures' of adequate functioning, we may limit freedom.

A further limitation is that this is a subjective judgement.

Someone has to judge whether a patient is distressed or distressing. Some patients may say they are distressed but may be judged as not suffering.

There are methods for making such judgements as objective as possible, including checklists such as the *Global Assessment of Functioning Scale*.

However, the principle remains whether someone, e.g. a psychiatrist, has the right to make this judgement.

One strength is that deviation from ideal mental health is comprehensive.

The definition covers a broad range of criteria for mental health.

It probably covers most of the reasons someone would seek help from mental health services or be referred for help.

The sheer range of factors discussed in relation to Jahoda's criteria make it a good tool for thinking about mental health.

One limitation is that the definition may be culturally relative.

Some of the ideas in Jahoda's classification of ideal mental health are specific to Western European and North American cultures.

For example, the emphasis on personal achievement (self-actualisation) would be considered self-indulgent in much of the world where the focus is on community rather than oneself.

Such traits are typical of **individualist** cultures and are culturally specific.

Another limitation is an unrealistically high standard for mental health.

Very few people will attain all Jahoda's criteria for mental health. Therefore, this approach would see most of us as abnormal.

On the positive side, it makes it clear to people the ways in which they could benefit from seeking help to improve their mental health.

However, it is probably of no value in thinking about who might benefit from treatment against their will.

Good luck with that, son. Some people have suggested that Jahoda's criteria might be a little unrealistic.

Phobias, depression and OCD

Spec spotlight

The behavioural, emotional and cognitive characteristics of phobias, depression and obsessive-compulsive disorder (OCD).

Genuphobia is fear of knees. Apologies if you're a sufferer.

Hippopotomonstrosesquipedaliophobia is fear of long words apparently. That's just mean isn't it?

Brian has been experiencing a lot of stress at work recently. He is lethargic and has no energy or enthusiasm for anything anymore. He can't concentrate on even the simplest tasks. He stares into space a lot just mulling over very negative thoughts, some of which make him anxious. He feels very down, finds it hard to get up in the morning and is eating more and putting on weight. Several times in the past month he has either been late for work or taken the day off.

Identify the behavioural, cognitive and emotional aspects of Brian's state.

Do you think he is suffering from depression? Explain your answer.

Explain why Brian is unlikely to be suffering from a phobia or OCD.

Phobias		
Behavioural	Panic.	
	This may involve a range of behaviours such as crying, screaming or running away from the phobic stimulus.	
	Avoidance.	
	Considerable effort to avoid coming into contact with the phobic stimulus. This can make it hard to go about everyday life, especially if the phobic stimulus is often seen, e.g. public places.	
Emotional	Anxiety and fear.	
	Fear is the immediate experience when a phobic encounters or thinks about the phobic stimulus. Fear leads to anxiety.	
	Responses are unreasonable.	
	Response is widely disproportionate to the threat posed, e.g. an arachnophobic will have a strong emotional response to a tiny spider.	
Cognitive	Selective attention to the phobic stimulus.	
	The phobic finds it hard to look away from the phobic stimulus e.g. a pogonophobic (fear of beards) cannot concentrate on a task if there is a bearded man in the room.	
	Irrational beliefs.	
	For example, social phobias may involve beliefs such as 'if I blush people will think I'm weak' or 'I must always sound intelligent'.	

Depression		
Behavioural	Activity levels.	
	Sufferers of depression have reduced levels of energy making them lethargic. In extreme cases, this can be so severe that the sufferer cannot get out of bed.	
	Disruption to sleep and eating behaviour.	
	Sufferers may experience reduced sleep (insomnia) or an increased need for sleep (hypersomnia).	
	Appetite may increase or decrease, leading to weight gain or loss.	
Cognitive	Poor concentration.	
	Sufferers may find themselves unable to stick with a task as they usually would, or they might find simple decision making difficult.	

Obsessive-compulsive disorder

Behavioural	**Compulsions.** Actions that are carried out repeatedly, e.g. handwashing. The same behaviour is repeated in a ritualistic way to reduce anxiety.
	Avoidance. The OCD is managed by avoiding situations that trigger anxiety, e.g. sufferers who wash repeatedly may avoid coming into contact with germs.
Emotional	**Anxiety and distress.** Obsessive thoughts are unpleasant and frightening, and the anxiety that goes with these can be overwhelming.
	Guilt and disgust. Irrational guilt, for example over a minor moral issue, or disgust which is directed towards oneself or something external like dirt.
Cognitive	**Obsessive thoughts.** About 90% of OCD sufferers have obsessive thoughts, e.g. recurring intrusive thoughts about being contaminated by dirt or germs.
	Insight into excessive anxiety. Awareness that thoughts and behaviour are irrational. In spite of this, sufferers experience catastrophic thoughts and are hypervigilant, i.e. 'over-aware' of their obsession.

Emotional	**Lowered mood.** More pronounced than the daily experience of feeling lethargic or sad. Sufferers often describe themselves as 'worthless' or 'empty'.
	Anger. On occasion, such emotions lead to aggression or self-harming behaviour.
	Absolutist thinking. 'Black and white thinking', when a situation is unfortunate it is seen as an absolute disaster.

REVISION BOOSTER

This spread deals with the characteristics of phobias, depression and OCD. Questions on this section are likely to be either descriptive or application. There isn't really scope for evaluative material here.

For each characteristic/symptom you describe, identify it clearly first before going on to describe it in detail. Use examples where you can.

KNOWLEDGE CHECK

1. Outline ways in which someone's emotional state may change in response to OCD. *(4 marks)*
2. Identify **one** emotional, **one** behavioural and **one** cognitive characteristic of OCD. *(3 marks)*
3. Explain characteristics of a phobia. *(6 marks)*
4. Explain cognitive **or** emotional characteristics of depression. *(4 marks)*
5. Outline the likely behavioural characteristics of someone who has been diagnosed with depression. *(6 marks)*

The behavioural approach to explaining phobias

Spec spotlight

The behavioural approach to explaining phobias: the two-process model, including classical and operant conditioning.

The behavioural approach is the same as behaviourism, which is described on page 72.

Phobia

Unconditioned stimulus ⟶	Unconditioned response
Being bitten	Anxiety
Neutral stimulus ⟶	No response
Dog	
Unconditioned + neutral stimulus ⟶	Unconditioned response
Being bitten + dog	Anxiety
Conditioned stimulus ⟶	Conditioned response
Dog	Anxiety

REVISION BOOSTER

If studies are used as evaluation, you should include very little description of procedures. But studies can also be used for descriptive content and then the procedures are relevant – here they act as an example of how classical conditioning works.

The Little Albert study. Some experts have questioned the authenticity of this photograph.

The two-process model

Classical conditioning and **operant conditioning**.	Orval Hobart Mowrer (1960) argued that phobias are learned by classical conditioning and then maintained by operant conditioning, i.e. two processes are involved.
Acquisition by classical conditioning.	Classical conditioning involves association. 1. **UCS** triggers a fear response (fear is a **UCR**), e.g. being bitten creates anxiety. 2. **NS** is associated with the UCS, e.g. being bitten by a dog (the dog previously did not create anxiety). 3. NS becomes a **CS** producing fear (which is now the **CR**). The dog becomes a CS causing a CR of anxiety/fear following the bite.
Little Albert: conditioned fear.	Watson and Raynor (1920) showed how a fear of rats could be conditioned in 'Little Albert'. 1. Whenever Albert played with a white rat, a loud noise was made close to his ear. The noise (UCS) caused a fear response (UCR). 2. Rat (NS) did not create fear until the bang and the rat had been paired together several times. 3. Albert showed a fear response (CR) every time he came into contact with the rat (now a CS).
Generalisation of fear to other stimuli.	For example, Little Albert also showed a fear in response to other white furry objects including a fur coat and a Santa Claus mask.
Maintenance by operant conditioning (negative reinforcement).	Operant conditioning takes place when our behaviour is reinforced or punished. Negative reinforcement – an individual produces behaviour that avoids something unpleasant. When a phobic avoids a phobic stimulus they escape the anxiety that would have been experienced. This reduction in fear negatively reinforces the avoidance behaviour and the phobia is maintained.
Example of negative reinforcement	If someone has a morbid fear of clowns (coulrophobia) they will avoid circuses and other situations where they may encounter clowns. The relief felt from avoiding clowns negatively reinforces the phobia and ensures it is maintained rather than confronted.

A strength of the two-process model is it has good explanatory power.

The two-process model went beyond Watson and Rayner's simple classical conditioning explanation of phobias.

It has important implications for therapy. If a patient is prevented from practising their avoidance behaviour then phobic behaviour declines.

The application to therapy is a strength of the two-process model.

There are alternative explanations for avoidance behaviour.

In more complex behaviours like agoraphobia, there is evidence that at least some avoidance behaviour is motivated more by positive feelings of safety.

This explains why some agoraphobics are able to leave their house with a trusted friend with relatively little anxiety, but not alone (Buck 2010).

This is a problem for the two-process model, which suggests that avoidance is motivated by anxiety reduction.

A limitation is the two-process model is an incomplete explanation of phobias.

Even if we accept that classical and operant conditioning are involved in the development and maintenance of phobias, there are some aspects of phobia behaviour that require further explaining.

We easily acquire phobias of things that were a danger in our evolutionary past (e.g. fear of snakes or the dark). This is *biological preparedness* – we are innately prepared to fear some things more than others (Seligman 1971).

The phenomenon of biological preparedness is a problem for the two-process model because it shows there is more to acquiring phobias than simple conditioning.

A limitation is that not all bad experiences lead to phobias.

Sometimes phobias do appear following a bad experience and it is easy to see how they could be the result of conditioning.

However, sometimes people have a bad experience (such as being bitten by a dog) and don't develop a phobia (DiNardo *et al.* 1988).

This suggests that conditioning alone cannot explain phobias. They may only develop where a vulnerability exists.

Two-process model doesn't properly consider the cognitive aspects of phobias.

We know that behavioural explanations in general are oriented towards explaining behaviour rather than cognition (thinking).

This is why the two-process model explains maintenance of phobias in terms of avoidance – but we also know that phobias have a cognitive element (see page 94).

The two-process theory does not adequately address the cognitive element of phobias.

Apply it

Marina has acrophobia, an irrational fear of heights. She hates even climbing the stairs at home and can't look out of the upstairs windows. Whenever Marina thinks about heights, she feels sick and starts sweating. She becomes very anxious in situations where she is aware of being 'off the ground', so she tries her best to avoid them but this is seriously interfering with her life.

Use the two-process model to explain how Marina's acrophobia was acquired and is maintained. In your explanation, refer to both classical and operant conditioning.

Explain **one** reason why this may not be an adequate explanation of Marina's acrophobia.

If you have agoraphobia and claustrophobia does that mean you can only cope with places that are medium-sized?

KNOWLEDGE CHECK

1. Explain the role of classical conditioning as used to explain the development of phobias. *(3 marks)*
2. Outline the two-process model of phobias. *(4 marks)*
3. Briefly evaluate the two-process model as an explanation for phobias. *(4 marks)*
4. Describe and evaluate the two-process model of phobias. Refer to the development and maintenance of a specific type of phobia as part of your answer. *(12 marks AS, 16 marks AL)*

The behavioural approach to treating phobias

Spec spotlight

The behavioural approach to treating phobias: systematic desensitisation including relaxation and use of hierarchy; flooding.

Apply it

Marina's acrophobia (fear of heights) is causing her such inconvenience and anxiety that she decides to get some help. She is referred to a clinical psychologist who uses systematic desensitisation to treat her phobia.

Explain practical ways in which each of the following would be included in Marina's treatment: (1) anxiety hierarchy, (2) relaxation, (3) exposure.

Marina isn't sure that systematic desensitisation is the best treatment for her phobia. Explain how she could be treated using an alternative behavioural therapy.

Not that kind of flooding. Unless you have a fear of water – in which case, welcome to the treatment room...

Systematic desensitisation (SD)

Based on **classical conditioning**, *counterconditioning* and *reciprocal inhibition*.	The therapy aims to gradually reduce anxiety through counterconditioning: • Phobia is learned so that phobic stimulus (**conditioned stimulus**, CS) produces fear (**conditioned response**, CR). • CS is paired with relaxation and this becomes the new CR. *Reciprocal inhibition* – it is not possible to be afraid and relaxed at the same time, so one emotion prevents the other.
Formation of an *anxiety hierarchy*.	Patient and therapist design an anxiety hierarchy – a list of fearful stimuli arranged in order from least to most frightening. An arachnophobic might identify seeing a picture of a small spider as low on their anxiety hierarchy and holding a tarantula as the final item.
Relaxation practised at each level of the hierarchy.	Phobic individual is first taught relaxation techniques such as deep breathing and/or meditation. Patient then works through the anxiety hierarchy. At each level the phobic is exposed to the phobic stimulus in a relaxed state. This takes place over several sessions starting at the bottom of the hierarchy. Treatment is successful when the person can stay relaxed in situations high on the hierarchy.

Flooding

Immediate exposure to the phobic stimulus.	Flooding involves bombarding the phobic patient with the phobic object without a gradual build-up. An arachnophobic receiving flooding treatment may have a large spider crawl over their hand until they can relax fully (the phobic not the spider)
Very quick learning through extinction.	Without the option of avoidance behaviour, the patient quickly learns that the phobic object is harmless through the exhaustion of their fear response. This is known as extinction.
Ethical safeguards.	Flooding is not unethical but it is an unpleasant experience so it is important that patients give **informed consent**. They must be fully prepared and know what to expect.

A strength of SD is that it is effective.

Gilroy *et al.* (2003) followed up 42 patients who had SD for spider phobia in three 45-minute sessions.

At both three and 33 months, the SD group were less fearful than a **control group** treated by relaxation without exposure.

This is a strength because it shows that SD is helpful in reducing the anxiety in spider phobia and that the effects of the treatment are long-lasting.

Another strength is that SD is suitable for a diverse range of patients.

The alternatives to SD such as flooding and **cognitive** therapies are not well suited to some patients.

For example, having learning difficulties can make it very hard for some patients to understand what is happening during flooding or to engage with cognitive therapies which require reflection.

For these patients, SD is probably the most appropriate treatment.

A further strength is that SD tends to be acceptable to patients.

A strength of SD is that patients prefer it. Those given the choice of SD or flooding tend to prefer SD.

This is because it does not cause the same degree of trauma as flooding. It may also be because SD includes some elements that are actually pleasant, such as time talking with a therapist.

This is reflected in the low refusal rates (number of patients refusing to start treatment) and low **attrition** rates (number of patients dropping out of treatment) for SD.

A limitation of flooding is that it is less effective for some types of phobia.

Although flooding is highly effective for treating simple phobias, it appears to be less so for more complex phobias like social phobias.

This may be because social phobias have cognitive aspects, e.g. a sufferer of social phobia doesn't simply experience anxiety but thinks unpleasant thoughts about the social situation.

This type of phobia may benefit more from cognitive therapies because such therapies tackle the irrational thinking.

A further limitation is that flooding is traumatic for patients.

Perhaps the most serious issue with the use of flooding is the fact that it is a highly traumatic experience.

The problem is not that flooding is unethical (patients do give informed consent) but that patients are often unwilling to see it through to the end.

This is a limitation because ultimately it means that the treatment is not effective, and time and money are wasted preparing patients only to have them refuse to start or complete treatment.

REVISION BOOSTER

There are two named treatments on the specification for the behavioural approach, so if both treatments are the focus of an essay, do not over-describe one at the expense of the other and don't spend too long on the description at the expense of the evaluation.

Comparison between treatments/ therapies is an excellent way to gain AO3 marks – and it's possible you may be asked to do this as part of an essay. Make a list of similarities and differences between systematic desensitisation and flooding and try to explain these in more detail.

It was at that point that Belinda wondered if the final stage of the anxiety hierarchy to cure her fear of the dentist had perhaps come a little too soon...

KNOWLEDGE CHECK

1. Outline **one** behavioural approach to treating phobias.
   (4 marks)

2. Identify and briefly discuss **one** limitation of flooding as a treatment for phobias.
   (4 marks)

3. Briefly evaluate flooding as a treatment for phobias. *(4 marks)*

4. Describe and evaluate **one or more** behavioural approaches to treating phobias.
   (12 marks AS, 16 marks AL)

The cognitive approach to explaining depression

Spec spotlight

The cognitive approach to explaining depression: Beck's negative triad and Ellis's ABC model.

Depression. Not a laughing matter – literally or metaphorically.

REVISION BOOSTER

The essay question you are most likely to be asked would be about the cognitive approach to explaining depression in general, rather then either Beck or Ellis alone. In such a case you should be careful not to spend too much time on description because the evaluation is at least as important as the description. However, it is possible that one essay might be on Beck or Ellis individually, so prepare that as well.

Rosie recently failed a mock A-level exam. She feels very down about it and is experiencing other symptoms of depression too. She thinks she is useless and worthless, and feels guilty for letting everyone down. She now finds she can't motivate herself to work or do anything to improve next time.

Explain Rosie's depression in terms of Beck's negative triad.

In Ellis's terms, identify and explain the ABC of Rosie's experience.

Beck's cognitive theory of depression

Faulty information processing.	Aaron Beck (1967) suggested that some people are more prone to depression because of faulty information processing, i.e. thinking in a flawed way.
	When depressed people attend to the negative aspects of a situation and ignore positives, they also tend to blow small problems out of proportion and think in 'black and white' terms.
Depressed people have negative self-*schemas*.	A *schema* is a 'package' of ideas and information developed through experience. We use schemas to interpret the world, so if a person has a negative self-schema they interpret *all* information about themselves in a negative way.
The *negative triad*.	There are three elements to the negative triad:

- *Negative views of the world*, e.g. 'the world is a cold hard place'.
- *Negative view of the future*, e.g. 'there isn't much chance that the economy will get any better'.
- *Negative view of the self*, e.g. thinking 'I am a failure' and this negatively impacts upon self-esteem.

Ellis's ABC model

A Activating event	Albert Ellis suggested that depression arises from *irrational thoughts*.
	According to Ellis depression occurs when we experience negative events, e.g. failing an important test or ending a relationship.
B Beliefs	Negative events trigger irrational beliefs, for example:

- Ellis called the belief that we *must always succeed* 'musterbation'.
- 'I-can't-stand-it-itis' is the belief that it is a disaster when things do not go smoothly.
- 'Utopianism' is the belief that the world must always be fair and just.

C Consequences	When an activating event triggers irrational beliefs there are emotional and behavioural consequences.
	For example, if you believe you must always succeed and then you fail at something, the consequence is depression.

A strength of Beck's theory is it has good supporting evidence.

For example, Grazioli and Terry (2000) assessed 65 pregnant women for **cognitive** vulnerability and depression before and after birth.

They found that those women judged to have been high in cognitive vulnerability were more likely to suffer post-natal depression.

These cognitions can be seen before depression develops, suggesting that Beck may be right about cognition causing depression, at least in some cases.

'I must succeed at everything'... 'Everyone must like me.' Ellis called this 'musterbating'. Be a bit careful how you write that in the exam.

Another strength is that the theory has practical application as a therapy.

Beck's cognitive explanation forms the basis of *cognitive behaviour therapy* (CBT).

The components of the negative triad can be easily identified and challenged in CBT. This means a patient can test whether the elements of the negative triad are true.

This is a strength of the explanation because it translates well into a successful therapy.

A limitation is that Beck's theory does not explain all aspects of depression.

Depression is a complex disorder. Some depressed patients are deeply angry and Beck cannot easily explain this extreme emotion.

Some depression patients suffer hallucinations and bizarre beliefs, or suffer *Cotard syndrome*, the delusion that they are zombies (Jarrett 2013).

Beck's theory cannot always explain all cases of depression, and just focuses on one aspect of the disorder.

A limitation is that Ellis's model is a partial explanation of depression.

There is no doubt that some cases of depression follow activating events.

Psychologists call this *reactive depression* and see it as different from the kind of depression that arises without an obvious cause.

This means that Ellis' explanation only applies to some kinds of depression.

A general issue is that cognitions may not cause all aspects of depression.

Cognitive explanations are closely tied up with the concept of cognitive primacy, the idea that emotions are influenced by cognition (your thoughts).

This is sometimes the case, but not necessarily always. Other theories of depression see emotions, such as anxiety and distress, as stored like physical energy, to emerge some time after their causal event.

This casts doubt on the idea that cognitions are always the root cause of depression and suggests that cognitive theories may not explain all aspects of the disorder.

KNOWLEDGE CHECK

1. Identify the **three** parts of Beck's negative triad and illustrate each with an example. *(6 marks)*

2. Outline the ABC model as an explanation for depression. *(4 marks)*

3. Evaluate the cognitive approach to explaining depression. *(6 marks)*

4. Maria recently failed her driving test. She says the test was unfair and the examiner was 'out to get her'. She says she hates herself and will never try anything again. Before the test Maria told her friend that she had to pass otherwise she could not go on. Maria's friend thinks she might be showing signs of depression.

   Describe and evaluate the cognitive approach to explaining depression. Refer to Maria in your answer. *(12 marks AS, 16 marks AL)*

The cognitive approach to treating depression

Spec spotlight

The cognitive approach to treating depression: cognitive behaviour therapy including challenging irrational thoughts.

REVISION BOOSTER

If you are asked to describe and evaluate the cognitive approach to treating depression, be careful not to include material on cognitive *explanations*. This is easily done – especially as the treatments are based on the assumptions of the explanations, but such material wouldn't get any credit.

Apply it

Rosie (from the previous spread) is being treated for depression by a cognitive behaviour therapist, who believes the key to successful treatment is to challenge Rosie's irrational thoughts.

Explain how the therapist might do this.

Rosie isn't sure how useful CBT is, so she comes to you for advice.

What would you tell her?

Ellis used to encourage his patients to take part in 'shame attacking exercises' such as taking a banana for a walk on a lead in a busy shopping centre. As his patients did so Ellis would remind them to think, 'What's the worst that could happen?'

Cognitive behaviour therapy (CBT)

Beck: Patient and therapist work together.	Patient and therapist: • Work together to clarify the patient's problems. • Identify where there might be negative or irrational thoughts that will benefit from challenge.
Challenging negative thoughts relating to negative triad.	The aim is to identify negative thoughts about the self, the world and the future – the negative triad. These thoughts must be challenged by the patient taking an active role in their treatment.
The 'patient as scientist'.	Patients are encouraged to test the reality of their irrational beliefs. They might be set homework, e.g. to record when they enjoyed an event or when people were nice to them. This is referred to as the 'patient as scientist'. In future sessions if patients say that no-one is nice to them or there is no point going on, the therapist can produce this evidence to prove the patient's beliefs incorrect.
Ellis's rational emotive behaviour therapy (*REBT*).	REBT extends the ABC model to an *ABCDE model*: • D for dispute (challenge) irrational beliefs. • E for effect.
Challenging irrational beliefs.	A patient might talk about how unlucky they have been or how unfair life is. An REBT therapist would identify this as utopianism and challenge it as an irrational belief. • Empirical argument – disputing whether there is evidence to support the irrational belief. • Logical argument – disputing whether the negative thought actually follows from the facts.
Behavioural activation.	As individuals become depressed, they tend to increasingly avoid difficult situations and become isolated, which maintains or worsens symptoms. The goal of treatment, therefore, is to work with depressed individuals to gradually decrease their avoidance and isolation, and increase their engagement in activities that have been shown to improve mood, e.g. exercising, going out to dinner, etc.

A strength of CBT is that it is effective.

There is a large body of evidence to support the effectiveness of CBT for depression, e.g. March *et al.* (2007) compared the effects of CBT with *antidepressant* drugs and a combination of the two in 327 depressed adolescents.

After 36 weeks 81% of the CBT group, 81% of the antidepressant group and 86% of the CBT + antidepressants group were significantly improved. CBT emerged as just as effective as medication and helpful alongside medication.

This suggests there is a good case for making CBT the first choice of treatment in public health care systems like the NHS.

A limitation of CBT is it may not work for the most severe cases of depression.

In some cases depression can be so severe that patients cannot motivate themselves to take on the hard **cognitive** work required for CBT.

Where this is the case it is possible to treat patients with antidepressant medication and commence CBT when they are more alert and motivated.

This is a limitation of CBT because it means CBT cannot be used as the sole treatment for all cases of depression.

Success may be due to the therapist–patient relationship.

Rosenzwieg (1936) suggested that the differences between various methods of psychotherapy might actually be quite small.

All psychotherapies have one essential ingredient – the relationship between therapist and patient. It may be the quality of this relationship that determines success rather than any particular technique.

Many comparative reviews (e.g. Luborsky *et al.* 2002) find very small differences between therapies, suggesting that they share a common basis.

A limitation is that some patients really want to explore their past.

One of the basic principles of CBT is that the focus of the therapy is on the patient's present and future, rather than their past.

In some other forms of psychotherapy patients make links between childhood experiences and current depression.

The 'present-focus' of CBT may ignore an important aspect of the depressed patient's experience.

Another limitation is that there may be an overemphasis on cognition.

CBT may end up minimising the importance of the circumstances in which the patient is living (McCusker 2014).

A patient living in poverty or suffering abuse needs to change their circumstances, and any approach that emphasises what is in the patient's mind rather than their environment can prevent this.

CBT techniques used inappropriately can demotivate people to change their situation.

REVISION BOOSTER

Note that some of these evaluation points apply to cognitive therapies in general rather than being specifically applied to Beck or Ellis. This is good as a shorter 'describe and evaluate' question – say *8 marks* – on Ellis or Beck would mean that you could use some of the same points in either case.

It may be the quality of the therapist–patient relationship that determines the success of therapy. Bad news for these two...

KNOWLEDGE CHECK

1. Explain **one** strength of using cognitive behaviour therapy to treat depression. *(3 marks)*
2. Explain how irrational thoughts are challenged as part of the cognitive approach to treating depression. *(3 marks)*
3. Outline and briefly discuss **one** cognitive approach to treating depression. *(6 marks)*
4. Describe and evaluate the cognitive approach to explaining depression and the cognitive approach to treating depression.
   (12 marks AS, 16 marks AL)

The biological approach to explaining OCD

Spec spotlight

The biological approach to explaining OCD: genetic and neural explanations.

Could an obsession with cleanliness be 'all in the genes'? Perhaps, judging by these two.

Apply it

Dilip is a middle-aged man who has OCD, especially intrusive thoughts about contamination. He wants to find out what causes it, and recalls that his dad used to compulsively wash himself and clean the house. Dilip is concerned that his children might also have OCD.

If you were to explain the genetic causes of OCD to Dilip, what would you tell him?

What else could you explain to Dilip about the role of the brain in OCD?

REVISION BOOSTER

There are two biological approaches to explaining OCD identified on the specification (genetic and neural). This means you could be set a question on biological approaches to explaining OCD in general or on each explanation specifically. We have only provided three AO1 points for each so you will need to ensure you make the most of these should separate essays be set.

Genetic explanations

Candidate *genes* e.g. 5HT1-D.	Researchers have identified specific genes which create a vulnerability for OCD, called candidate genes.
	• **Serotonin** genes, e.g.5HT1-D beta, are implicated in the transmission of serotonin across *synapses*.
	• **Dopamine** genes are also implicated in OCD.
	Both dopamine and serotonin are *neurotransmitters* that have a role in regulating mood.
OCD is polygenic.	OCD is not caused by one single gene but several genes are involved.
	Taylor (2013) found evidence that up to 230 different genes may be involved in OCD.
Different types of OCD.	One group of genes may cause OCD in one person but a different group of genes may cause the disorder in another person – known as *aetiologically heterogeneous*.
	There is also evidence that different types of OCD may be the result of particular genetic variations, such as hoarding disorder and religious obsession.

Neural explanations

Low levels of serotonin lowers mood.	Neurotransmitters are responsible for relaying information from one *neuron* to another.
	For example if a person has low levels of serotonin then normal transmission of mood-relevant information does not take place and mood (and sometimes other mental processes) is affected.
Decision-making systems in *frontal lobes* impaired.	Some cases of OCD, and in particular hoarding disorder, seem to be associated with impaired decision making.
	This is turn may be associated with abnormal functioning of the lateral (the side bits) frontal lobes of the brain.
	The frontal lobes are responsible for logical thinking and making decisions.
Parahippocampal gyrus dysfunctional.	There is also evidence to suggest that an area called the left parahippocampal gyrus associated with processing unpleasant emotions, functions abnormally in OCD.

There is good supporting evidence for the genetic explanation of OCD.

There is evidence from a variety of sources which suggests that some people are vulnerable to OCD as a result of their genetic make-up.

For example, Nestadt et al. (2010) reviewed twin studies and found that 68% of identical twins (MZ) shared OCD as opposed to 31% of non-identical (DZ) twins

This strongly supports a genetic influence on OCD.

One limitation is that too many candidate genes have been identified.

Twin studies strongly suggest that OCD is largely genetic, but psychologists have been less successful at pinning down all the genes involved.

One reason for this is that it appears that several genes are involved and that each genetic variation only increases the risk of OCD by a fraction.

The consequence is that a genetic explanation is unlikely to ever be very useful because it provides little predictive value.

Another limitation is that environmental risk factors are also involved.

It is not just genes, but it seems that environmental risk factors can also trigger or increase the risk of developing OCD.

For example, Cromer et al. (2007) found that over half the OCD patients in their sample had a traumatic event in their past, and OCD was more severe in those with one or more traumas.

This supports the diathesis-stress model. Focusing on environmental causes may be more productive because we are more able to do something about these.

We all have our little obsessions... but when they lead to repetitive behaviour is when it becomes an illness.

There is some supporting evidence for neural explanations of OCD.

Antidepressants that work purely on the serotonin system are effective in reducing OCD symptoms and this suggests that the serotonin system may be involved in OCD.

Also, OCD symptoms form part of biological conditions such as *Parkinson's Disease* (Nestasdt et al. 2010).

This suggests that the biological processes that cause the symptoms in those conditions may also be responsible for OCD.

One limitation is that the serotonin-OCD link may not be unique to OCD.

Many people who suffer from OCD become depressed. Having two disorders together is called *co-morbidity.*

This depression probably involves (though is not necessarily caused by) disruption to the serotonin system. This leaves us with a logical problem when it comes to the serotonin system as a possible basis for OCD.

It could simply be that the serotonin system is disrupted in many patients with OCD because they are depressed as well.

KNOWLEDGE CHECK

1. Explain the genetic or neural explanation for OCD. *(4 marks)*
2. Explain **one** criticism of the neural explanation for OCD. *(3 marks)*
3. Outline the biological approach to explaining OCD. *(4 marks)*
4. Describe and evaluate research into genetic and neural explanations of OCD. *(12 marks AS, 16 marks AL)*

The biological approach to treating OCD

Spec spotlight

The biological approach to treating OCD: drug therapy.

Ironic that OCD is classed as a 'disorder'. It's all about order.

REVISION BOOSTER

Six marks' worth of description on drug therapy is quite demanding. For this reason, you should include reference to named examples (as we have here) as well as their specific 'mode of action' (i.e. what they do) in the brain.

Apply it

Dilip eventually visits his GP for help with his OCD. The GP recommends a psychological therapy but Dilip is adamant that he does not want that kind of treatment and wonders if there is a drug he can take instead.

Identify which drug Dilip's GP is likely to prescribe and suggest how the doctor might explain how the drug will work to treat OCD.

Outline **one** argument Dilip's GP might use to persuade him to reconsider his opposition to psychological treatment.

'When you're obsessive, like me, searching for something unattainable can become unhealthy... it's like falling through the air and grabbing at the clouds'

— *Jonny Wilkinson, rugby player.*

Drug therapy

Changing levels of *neurotransmitters*.	Drug therapy for mental disorders aims to increase or decrease levels of neurotransmitters in the brain or to increase/decrease their activity.
	Low levels of **serotonin** are associated with OCD.
	Therefore drugs work in various ways to increase the level of serotonin in the brain.
Selective serotonin reuptake inhibitor (SSRIs).	SSRIs prevent the reabsorption and breakdown of serotonin in the brain. This increases its levels in the synapse and thus serotonin continues to stimulate the *postsynaptic neuron*.
	This compensates for whatever is wrong with the serotonin system in OCD.
Typical dosage	A typical daily dose of *Fluoxetine* (an SSRI) is 20mg although this may be increased if it is not benefitting the patient.
	It takes 3–4 months of daily use for SSRIs to impact upon symptoms.
	This can be increased (e.g. 60mg a day) if this is appropriate.
Combining SSRIs with CBT.	Drugs are often used alongside *cognitive behaviour therapy* (CBT) to treat OCD.
	The drugs reduce a patient's emotional symptoms, such as feeling anxious or depressed. This means that patients can engage more effectively with CBT.
Alternatives to SSRIs: *Tricyclics*.	Tricyclics (an older type of antidepressant) are sometimes used, such as *Clomipramine*.
	These have the same effect on the serotonin system as SSRIs but the side-effects can be more severe.
Alternatives to SSRIs: *SNRIs*.	In the last five years a different class of antidepressant drugs called serotonin *noradrenaline reuptake inhibitor* (SNRIs) has also been used to treat OCD.
	Like tricyclics these are a second line of defence for patients who don't respond to SSRIs.
	SNRIs increase levels of serotonin as well as *noradrenaline*.

A strength of drug therapy is that it is effective at tackling OCD symptoms.

For example, Soomro *et al.* (2009) reviewed 17 studies comparing SSRIs to *placebos* in the treatment of OCD. All 17 studies showed significantly better results for SSRIs than for the placebo conditions.

Effectiveness is greatest when SSRIs are combined with a psychological treatment, usually CBT.

Typically symptoms reduce for around 70% of patients taking SSRIs, the rest are helped by alternative drugs or CBT+drugs. So drugs can help most patients with OCD.

'I do not have OCD, OCD, OCD' –

Emilie Autumn.

Another strength is that drugs are cost-effective and non-disruptive.

A strength of drug treatments in general is that they are cheap compared to psychological treatments. Using drugs to treat OCD is therefore good value for the NHS.

As compared to psychological therapies, SSRIs are also non-disruptive to patients' lives. If you wish you can simply take drugs until your symptoms decline and not engage with the hard work of psychological therapy.

Many doctors and patients like drug treatments for these reasons.

A limitation is that drugs can have side-effects.

Although drugs such as SSRIs help most people, a small minority will get no benefit. Some patients also suffer side-effects such as indigestion, blurred vision and loss of sex drive (although these side-effects are usually temporary).

For those taking *Clomipramine*, side-effects are more common and can be more serious. More than 1 in 10 patients suffer erection problems and weight gain, 1 in 100 become aggressive and suffer disruption to blood pressure and heart rhythm.

Such factors reduce effectiveness because people stop taking the medication.

Apparently chocolate can increase levels of serotonin in the brain – 'I'll take one large dose three times a day please doctor...'

A further limitation is the evidence for drug treatments is unreliable.

Although SSRIs are fairly effective and any side-effects will probably be short term, like all drug treatments, SSRIs have some controversy attached.

For example, some believe the evidence favouring drug treatments is biased because it is sponsored by drug companies who do not report all evidence (Goldacre 2013).

Such companies may try to suppress evidence that does not support the effectiveness of certain drugs to maximise their economic gain.

1. Outline the use of drug therapy for OCD. *(4 marks)*
2. Explain **two** criticisms of using drug therapy to treat OCD. *(6 marks)*
3. Outline and briefly evaluate drug therapy as a treatment for OCD. *(6 marks)*
4. Describe and evaluate the biological approach to treating OCD. *(12 marks AS, 16 marks AL)*

One problem is that some cases of OCD follow trauma.

OCD is widely believed to be biological in origin. It makes sense therefore that the standard treatment should be biological.

However, it is acknowledged that OCD can have a range of other causes, and that in some cases it is a response to traumatic life events.

It may not be appropriate to use drugs when treating cases that follow a trauma when psychological therapies may provide the best option.

Experimental method

Spec spotlight

Aims: stating aims; the difference between aims and hypotheses.

Hypotheses: directional and non-directional.

Experimental method.

Variables: including independent and dependent; operationalisation of variables. Extraneous and confounding variables.

Demand characteristics and investigator effects. Randomisation and standardisation.

Experimental designs: repeated measures, independent groups, matched pairs.

In an experiment into forgetting, two groups of participants learned a list of ten words. Each group was then given a new list to learn – either synonyms (words with the same meanings as those in the original list) or nonsense syllables (e.g. CEZ). Both groups then recalled the words from the original list.

1. Write a suitable hypothesis for this study. *(2 marks)*
2. State the operationalised IV and DV for this study. *(2 marks)*
3. Explain how demand characteristics might have influenced this study. *(2 marks)*
4. Explain how randomisation could have been used in this study. *(2 marks)*

The term 'research technique' refers to set of procedures used to collect data as part of psychological research. In some investigations, more than one technique may be used – such as the use of questionnaires to measure the DV in an experiment. Read on....

Key concepts

Aim	A general expression of what the researcher intends to investigate.
Hypothesis	A statement of what the researcher believes to be true. It should be *operationalised*, i.e. clearly defined and measurable. A directional *hypothesis* states whether changes are greater or lesser, positive or negative, etc. A *non-directional hypothesis* doesn't state the direction, just that there is a difference, correlation, association.
Experimental method	A researcher causes the *independent variable* (IV) to vary and records the effect of the IV on the *dependent variable* (DV). There are different *levels* of the IV.

Research issues

Extraneous and confounding variables	• *Extraneous variables* (EVs) are 'nuisance' variables that do not vary systematically with the IV. A researcher may control some of these. • *Confounding variables* (CVs) change systematically with the IV so we cannot be sure if any observed change in the DV is due to the CV or the IV. CVs must be controlled.
Demand characteristics	Refers to any cue from the researcher or research situation that may reveal the aim of the study.
Investigator effects	Any effect of the investigator's behaviour on the outcome of the research (the DV).

Research techniques

Randomisation	The use of chance when designing investigations to control for the effects of bias.
Standardisation	Using exactly the same formalised procedures for all participants in a research study.
Control groups	Control groups are used for the purpose of setting a comparison. They act as a 'baseline' and help establish causation.
Single blind and double blind	Single blind – a participant doesn't know the aims of the study so that demand characteristics are reduced. Double blind – both participant and researcher don't know the aims of the study to reduce demand characteristics and investigator effects.

Independent groups

One group do condition A and a second group do condition B.

Participants should be **randomly allocated** to **experimental groups**.

⊕ No order effects.	Participants are only tested once so can't practise or become bored/tired.	This controls an important CV.
⊕ Will not guess aim.	Participants only tested once so are unlikely to guess the research aims.	Therefore behaviour may be more 'natural'.
⊖ Participant variables.	The participants in the two groups are different, acting as EV/CV.	May reduce the **validity** of the study.
⊖ More participants.	Need twice as many participants as repeated measures for same data.	More time spent recruiting which is expensive.

Repeated measures

Same participants take part in all conditions of an experiment.

The order of conditions should be *counterbalanced* to avoid order effects.

⊕ Participant variables.	The person in both conditions has the same characteristics.	This controls an important CV.
⊕ Fewer participants.	Half the number of participants is needed than in independent groups.	Less time spent recruiting participants.
⊖ Order effects are a problem.	Participants may do better or worse when doing a similar task twice.	Reduces the validity of the results.
⊖ Participants may guess aims.	Participants may change their behaviour.	This may reduce the validity of the results.

Matched pairs

Two groups of participants are used but they are also related to each other by being paired on *participant variable*(s) that matter for the experiment.

⊕ Participant variables.	Participants matched on a variable that is relevant to the experiment.	This enhances the validity of the results.
⊕ No order effects.	Participants are only tested once so no practice or fatigue effects.	This enhances the validity of the results.
⊖ Matching is not perfect.	Matching is time-consuming and can't control all relevant variables.	May not address *participant variables*.
⊖ More participants.	Need twice as many participants as repeated measures for same data.	More time spent recruiting which is expensive.

Participant variables may act as confounding variables in an independent groups designs because people in each condition are different. This may be the cause of the change in the DV – rather than the manipulation of the IV.

Order effects come about when participants are tested more than once – as in repeated measures designs. This might lead to better performance through practice, or worse performance due to boredom or fatigue.

Trevor and Mervyn are often mistaken for identical twins – but incredibly, there is an 11-year age gap.

REVISION BOOSTER

Remember that even though, in a matched pairs design, there has been some attempt to control for participant variables, there are inevitably differences (even between identical twins), so participant variables may still be a problem.

KNOWLEDGE CHECK

1. Explain what is meant by the term 'directional hypothesis'. *(2 marks)*
2. Explain the difference between an extraneous and a confounding variable. *(3 marks)*
3. Outline what is meant by the term 'investigator effects'. Explain why these should be controlled in a research study. *(2 marks + 2 marks)*
4. Explain **one** strength of a repeated measures design. *(2 marks)*

Types of experiment

Spec spotlight

Types of experiment, laboratory and field experiments; natural and quasi- experiments.

Apply it

Identify the type of experiment (lab, field, natural or quasi) described below. **(1 mark each)**

1. Investigating whether older (over 50) or younger people (under 30) are more likely to binge drink alcohol.
2. Comparing the number of 'treats' received on Halloween by children dressed in 'scary' costumes or in everyday clothes.
3. Measuring how many words from a list people could remember when presented with cues such as category names.
4. Measuring the change in stress levels of people in an affected area before and after an earthquake.

Ben had been stood there for four and a half hours. It was only then he realised that he may have misunderstood his psychology teacher's suggestion that he go out and perform a field study.

Laboratory experiment

A controlled environment where **extraneous** and **confounding variables** (EVs and CVs) can be regulated.

Participants go to researcher.

The **IV** is manipulated and the effect on the **DV** is recorded.

⊕ EVs and CVs can be controlled.	This means that the effect of EVs and CVs on the DV can be minimised.	Cause and effect between the IV and DV can be demonstrated (high **internal validity**).
⊕ Can be easily **replicated**.	Due to the **standardised** procedure the experiment can be repeated.	If the results are the same this confirms their **validity**.
⊖ May lack **generalisability**.	The controlled lab environment may be rather artificial and participants are aware they are being studied.	Thus behaviour may not be 'natural' and can't be generalised to everyday life (low **external validity**).
⊖ **Demand characteristics** may be a problem.	These are cues in the experimental situation that invite a particular response from participants.	The results of the experiment may be explained by these cues rather than the effect of the IV.

Field experiment

A natural setting.

The researcher goes to participants.

The IV is manipulated and the effect on the DV is recorded.

⊕ More natural environment.	Participants more comfortable in their own environment.	Results may be more generalisable to everyday.
⊕ Participants are unaware of being studied.	They are more likely to behave as they normally do so the findings can be generalised.	The study has greater external validity.
⊖ More difficult to control CVs.	Observed changes in the DV may not be due to the IV, but to CVs instead.	It is more difficult to establish cause and effect than in the lab.
⊖ There are ethical issues.	Participants in a field experiment may not have given **informed consent**.	This is an invasion of participants' privacy, which raises ethical issues.

Natural experiment

The experimenter does not manipulate the IV. The IV would have varied even if the experimenter wasn't interested.

DV may be naturally occurring (e.g. exam results) or may be measured by the experimenter.

⊕ May be the only ethical option.	It may be unethical to manipulate the IV, e.g. studying the effects of institutionalisation on children.	A natural experiment may be the only way causal research can be done for such topics.
⊕ Greater external validity.	Natural experiments involve real-life issues, such as the effect of a natural disaster on stress levels.	This means the findings are more relevant to real experiences.
⊖ The natural event may only occur rarely.	Many natural events are 'one-offs' and this reduces the opportunity for research.	This may limit the scope for generalising findings to other similar situations.
⊖ Participants are not **randomly allocated**.	The experimenter has no control over which participants are placed in which condition as the IV is pre-existing.	May result in CVs that aren't controlled, e.g. Romanian orphans adopted early may also be the friendlier ones.

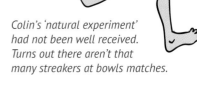

Colin's 'natural experiment' had not been well received. Turns out there aren't that many streakers at bowls matches.

Natural experiments are not necessarily natural at all. A study might involve a comparison between football players and rugby players (IV varies 'naturally'). The DV could be an IQ test measured in a controlled lab environment. IQ tests aren't that natural.

Quasi-experiment

IV is based on a pre-existing difference between people, e.g. age or gender. No one has manipulated this variable, it simply exists.

DV may be naturally occurring (e.g. exam results) or may be measured by the experimenter.

⊕ There is often high control.	Often carried out under controlled conditions and therefore shares some of the strengths of lab experiments.	This means increased confidence about drawing causal conclusions.
⊕ Comparisons can be made between people.	In a quasi-experiment the IV is a difference between people, e.g. people with and without autism.	This means that comparisons between different types of people can be made.
⊖ Participants are not randomly allocated.	The experimenter has no control over which participants are placed in which condition as the IV is pre-existing.	*Participant variables* may have caused the change in the DV acting as a CV.
⊖ Causal relationships not demonstrated.	The researcher does not manipulate/control the IV.	We cannot say for certain that any change in the DV was due to the IV.

KNOWLEDGE CHECK

1. Explain what is meant by a 'field experiment'. (2 marks)
2. Explain **one** strength and **one** limitation of a laboratory experiment. (2 marks + 2 marks)
3. Explain the difference between a field experiment and a natural experiment. (3 marks)
4. Consider the strengths and weaknesses of a quasi-experiment. (4 marks)

Sampling

Spec spotlight

Sampling: the difference between population and sample; sampling techniques including random, systematic, stratified, opportunity and volunteer; implications of sampling techniques, including bias and generalisation.

REVISION BOOSTER

It is important to note that 'sampling' is a term that's used in a couple of different ways when discussing research. As well as referring to ways in which participants are selected for studies (as on this spread) it's also a way of 'structuring' data collection in an observation – see 'time sampling' and 'event sampling' on page 117.

Mustard

Volunteer samples can be unrepresentative as they tend to attract people who are keen, curious and overly helpful. As keen as mustard in fact! Hence the mustard. Keep up.

Population and sample

Population	The large group of people that a researcher is interested in studying, for example college students from the North West.
Sample	It is usually not possible to include all members of the population in the study, so a smaller group is selected – the *sample*.
Generalisation	The sample that is drawn should be representative of the population so **generalisations** can be made.
Bias	The majority of samples are biased in that certain groups may be over- or under-represented.

Opportunity sample

Most available	People who are simply most available, i.e. the ones who are nearest/easiest to obtain.	
How?	Ask people nearby, e.g. ask the students in your class to take part or ask people who walk past you at a shopping centre.	
⊕ Quick method	Opportunity sampling is convenient because you just make use of the people who are closest.	This makes it one of the most popular sampling methods.
⊖ Inevitably biased	The sample is unrepresentative of the target population as it is drawn from a very specific area, such as one street in one town.	This means that the findings cannot be generalised.

Volunteer sample

Self-selecting	In a volunteer sample, participants select themselves.	
How?	Advertise. For example, place an ad in a newspaper or on a noticeboard and participants come to you.	
⊕ Participants are willing	Participants have selected themselves and know how much time and effort is involved.	Likely to engage more than people stopped in the street.
⊖ Likely to be a biased sample	Participants may share certain traits, e.g. keen and curious.	Generalisation limited due to volunteer bias.

Random sample

Equal chance	Every person in the target population has an equal chance of being selected.	
How?	Lottery method. All members of the target population are given a number and placed in a hat or tombola.	
⊕ Potentially unbiased	The researcher has no influence over who is selected.	Free from researcher bias.
⊖ Representation not guaranteed	Still possible that a random method may produce a biased sample.	Limits ability to generalise.

The National Lottery – the ultimate random method and a 1 in 14 million chance of winning!

Face facts my friend – it's never gonna happen...

Systematic sample

Sampling frame	Participants are selected using a set 'pattern' (sampling frame).	
How?	Every *nth* person is selected from a list of the target population.	
⊕ Unbiased	The first item is usually selected at random.	Objective method.
⊖ Time and effort	A complete list of the population is required.	May as well use random sampling.

Stratified sample

Frequency	Participants are selected according to their frequency in the target population.	
How?	Subgroups (or 'strata') are identified, such as gender or age groups. The relative percentages of the subgroups in the population are reflected in the sample.	
⊕ Representative method.	The characteristics of the target population are represented.	Generalisability more likely than other methods.
⊖ Stratification is not perfect.	Strata cannot reflect all the ways in which people are different.	Complete representation is not possible.

Apply it

Two psychologists wanted to study caregiver–child interactions using the Strange Situation. They needed to recruit 50 caregivers (and their babies), and decided to use random sampling.

1. Explain how they could obtain a random sample of caregivers from their local area. *(3 marks)*
2. Another psychologist points out that it would be easier to use a volunteer sample. Explain why. *(2 marks)*
3. Explain why volunteer sampling would probably produce a biased sample. *(2 marks)*

KNOWLEDGE CHECK

1. Explain the difference between a population and a sample. *(3 marks)*
2. Explain what is meant by 'random sampling'. *(2 marks)*
3. Outline **one** strength and **one** limitation of systematic sampling. *(2 marks +2 marks)*
4. Explain how you could select a stratified sample of male and female students within a school or college. *(3 marks)*
5. Explain **one** reason why generalisation from an opportunity sample would be difficult. *(2 marks)*

Ethical issues and ways of dealing with them

Spec spotlight

Ethics, including the role of the BPS code of ethics; ethical issues in the design and conduct of psychological studies; dealing with ethical issues in research.

A researcher investigated the effectiveness of a new anti-depressant drug. She randomly allocated participants diagnosed with depression to a treatment group (the new drug) or a control group (a placebo).

1. Explain **two** ethical issues that could have arisen in this study. *(2 marks + 2 marks)*
2. Outline how the psychologist could have dealt with each issue. *(2 marks + 2 marks)*

KNOWLEDGE CHECK

1. Using an example from psychological research, explain what is meant by the term 'ethical issue'. *(3 marks)*
2. Identify **one** ethical issue in psychological research. Outline **one** way in which this issue can be dealt with. *(1 mark + 2 marks)*
3. Outline the role of the BPS code of ethics in psychological research. *(4 marks)*

Ethical issues

Conflict	When a conflict exists between the rights of participants and the aims of the research.	*BPS code of conduct* is a quasi-legal document to protect participants based on four principles: *respect, competence, responsibility* and *integrity*. *Ethics committees* weigh up costs (e.g. potential harm) and *benefits* (e.g. value of research) before deciding whether a study should go ahead.

Informed consent

Get permission	Participants should be able to make an informed judgement about whether to take part.	Too much information may affect participants' behaviour so alternative forms of consent are: • *Presumptive* – ask a similar group. • *Prior general* – agree to be deceived. • *Retrospective* – get consent after the study.

Deception

Misleading	Deliberately misleading or withholding information so consent is not informed.	At the end of a study, participants should be given a *debrief* where they are advised of: 1. The true aims of the investigation. 2. Details that were not given during the study, e.g. existence of other groups or conditions. 3. What their data will be used for. 4. Their right to withhold data.

Protection from harm

Risk	Participants should be at no more risk than they would be in everyday life.	• Should be given the *right to withdraw* at each stage of the research process. • Should be reassured that their behaviour was typical/normal during the debriefing. • Researcher should provide *counselling* if participants have been, e.g. distressed.

Privacy/confidentiality

Right to control	We have the right to control information about ourselves. If this is invaded, confidentiality should be respected.	• If personal details are held these must be protected (a legal requirement). Usually though, no personal details are recorded. • Researchers refer to participants using numbers, initials or false names. • Participants' personal data cannot be shared with other researchers.

Association	Illustrates the strength and direction of an association between two co-variables.
Scattergram	Correlations are plotted on a scattergram. One co-variable is on the x-axis, the other is on the y-axis.
Types of correlation	• *Positive correlation* – co-variables rise or fall together. • *Negative correlation* – one co-variable rises and the other falls. • *Zero correlation* – no relationship between the two variables.

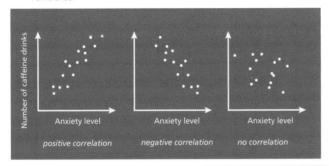

Differences between correlations and experiments	• In an experiment the researcher manipulates the IV and records the effect on the DV. In a correlation there is no manipulation of variables and so *cause and effect* cannot be demonstrated. • In a correlation the influence of EVs is not controlled, so it may be that a third 'untested' variable is causing the relationship between the co-variables (called an *intervening variable*).	
⊕ Useful starting point for research.	By assessing the strength and direction of a relationship, correlations provide a precise measure of how two variables are related.	If variables are strongly related it may suggest hypotheses for future research.
⊕ Relatively economical.	Unlike a lab study, there is no need for a controlled environment and no manipulation of variables is required.	Correlations are less time-consuming than experiments.
⊖ No cause and effect.	Correlations are often presented as causal, e.g. by the media, when they only show how two variables are related.	There may be intervening variables that explain the relationship.
⊖ Method used to measure variables may be flawed.	For example, the method used to work out an aggression score might be low in **reliability** (observational categories might have been used).	This would reduce the **validity** of the correlational study.

A psychologist investigated a disorder known as seasonal affective disorder (SAD). He found that as the number of daylight hours increased in the spring, participants in the study became less depressed.

Is this a positive, negative or zero correlation? Explain your answer.
(3 marks)

There is apparently a strong positive correlation between the number of ice creams eaten on a particular day and the number of cases of drowning.

Are ice creams that dangerous?! Or could there be a third 'intervening' variable? Hmm.

KNOWLEDGE CHECK

1. Explain what is meant by the term 'co-variable'. *(2 marks)*
2. Explain **one** difference between a correlation and an experiment. *(2 marks)*
3. Explain **one** strength and **one** limitation of using correlations in psychological research. *(2 marks + 2 marks)*

Observation

Spec spotlight

Observational techniques. Types of observation: naturalistic and controlled; covert and overt; participant and non participant.

Observational design: behavioural categories; event sampling, time sampling.

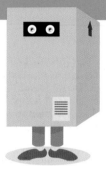

Several of Benedict's fellow researchers had pointed out that his covert observation disguise wasn't quite as brilliant as he thought it was.

Apply it

A psychologist studying stages of attachment observed infants in their own homes. He was especially interested in how much stranger anxiety the children showed in response to his presence.

1. Explain how this observation study could be described as (a) naturalistic, (b) overt and (c) participant observation.
   (2 marks + 2 marks + 2 marks)
2. Outline **one** strength and **one** limitation of this study as a naturalistic observation.
   (2 marks + 2 marks)
3. Identify **two** behavioural categories the psychologist could use to measure stranger anxiety. *(1 mark + 1 mark)*
4. Explain how the psychologist could have used time sampling in this study. *(2 marks)*

Observational techniques

A way of seeing or listening to what people do without having to ask them. Observation is often used within an experiment as a way of assessing the *DV*.

⊕ Can capture unexpected behaviour.	People often act differently from how they say they will in self-report methods.	Observations are useful as they give insight into spontaneous behaviour.
⊖ Risk of observer bias.	Researcher's interpretation of the situation may be affected by expectations.	Bias can be reduced using more than one observer.

Naturalistic – takes place where the target behaviour would normally occur.

⊕ High **external validity**.	In a natural context, behaviour is likely to be more spontaneous.	More **generalisable** to everyday life.
⊖ Low control.	There may be uncontrolled EVs.	Makes it more difficult to detect patterns.

Controlled – some control/manipulation of variables including control of EVs.

⊕ Can be **replicated**.	More easily repeated due to **standardised** procedures.	Findings can be checked to see if they occur again.
⊖ May have low external validity.	Behaviour may be contrived as a result of the setting.	Findings cannot be applied to everyday experience.

Covert – participants are unaware they are being studied.

⊕ **Demand characteristics** reduced.	Participants do not know they are being watched so their behaviour will be more natural.	This increases the validity of the findings.
⊖ Ethically questionable.	People may not want behaviour recorded, even in public.	Participants' right to privacy may be affected.

Overt – participants are aware of being studied.

⊕ More ethically acceptable.	Participants have given their consent to be studied.	They have the right to withdraw if they wish.
⊖ Demand characteristics.	Knowledge of being studied influences behaviour.	Reduces the validity of the findings.

Participant – when the researcher becomes part of the group they are studying.

⊕ Can lead to greater insight.	Researcher experiences the situation as the participants do.	This enhances the validity of the findings.
⊖ Possible loss of objectivity.	The researcher may identify too strongly with those they are studying ('going native').	This threatens the objectivity and validity of the findings.

Non-participant – when the researcher remains separate from the group they are studying.

⊕ More objective.	Researcher maintains an objective distance so less chance of bias.	May increase the validity of the findings.
⊖ Loss of insight.	Researcher may be too far removed from those they are studying.	May reduce the validity of the findings.

Observational design

Behavioural categories – the target behaviour to be observed should be broken up into a set of observable categories. This is similar to the idea of *operationalisation*.

⊖ Difficult to make clear and unambiguous.	Categories should be self-evident and not overlap, not always possible to achieve.	'Smiling' and 'grinning' would be poor categories.
⊖ Dustbin categories.	All forms of behaviour should be in the list and not one 'dustbin'.	'Dumped' behaviours go unrecorded.

Time sampling – observations are made at regular intervals, e.g. once every 15 seconds.

⊕ Reduces the number of observations.	Rather than recording everything that is seen (i.e. continuous) data is recorded at certain intervals.	The observation is more structured and systematic.
⊖ May be unrepresentative.	The researcher may miss important details outside of the time-scale.	May not reflect the whole behaviour.

Event sampling – a target behaviour/event is recorded every time it occurs.

⊕ May record infrequent behaviour.	The researcher will still 'pick up' behaviours that do not occur at regular intervals.	Such behaviours could easily be missed using time sampling.
⊖ Complex behaviour oversimplified.	If the event is too complex, important details may go unrecorded.	This may affect the **validity** of the findings.

That'll be a non-participant observation then.

Unstructured observation – everything is recorded which can be quite difficult if a lot is going on.

Structured observation includes behavioural categories and sampling methods.

A naturalistic observation often uses structured design.

REVISION BOOSTER

In an observational study, the researcher decides:

- *Who* to sample using sampling methods such as volunteer or opportunity.
- *How* the behaviours are sampled using time or event sampling.

For example, observing whether male or female drivers are more likely to 'jump' a red light would most likely involve opportunity and then event sampling.

KNOWLEDGE CHECK

1. Outline the difference between naturalistic and controlled observation. *(3 marks)*
2. Explain what is meant by 'covert observation'. *(2 marks)*
3. Explain **one** strength and **one** limitation of participant observation. *(2 marks + 2 marks)*

Self-report techniques

Spec spotlight

Self-report techniques:
questionnaires; interviews,
structured and unstructured

Questionnaire construction,
including use of open and closed
questions; design of interviews.

*All self-report techniques are used
to assess what people think and/
or feel.*

*Many questionnaires make use of
rating scales where respondents
are asked to indicate how strongly
they feel about a particular topic
or issue (perhaps on a scale of 1
to 7) or through a set of verbal
designations, such as strongly
agree, agree, undecided, disagree,
strongly disagree (called a **Likert
scale**).*

*As the only interviewee, Norman felt
he had an excellent chance of getting
the job. Unfortunately – as would
become all too clear six hours later –
he had turned up on the wrong day.*

*There is a danger of **interviewer
bias** in interviews. The interviewer
may encourage the interviewee to
explore certain topics and lines
of enquiry when the interaction
is `free-flowing'. This is why most
interviews benefit from a clearly
defined **interview schedule** (see
facing page).*

*Also, at the analysis stage, the
conclusions that are drawn may
be due to the subjective (biased)
interpretation of the researcher.*

Questionnaires

Questionnaires are made up of a pre-set list of written questions (or items) to which a participant responds.

They can be used as part of an *experiment* to assess the *DV*.

⊕ Can be distributed to lots of people.	Can gather large amounts of data quickly and the researcher need not be present when completed.	Reduces the effort involved and makes questionnaires cost-effective.
⊕ Respondents may be willing to 'open up'.	Respondents may share more personal information than in an interview as they are less self-conscious.	There may be less chance of *social desirability bias* compared to an interview.
⊖ Responses may not always be truthful.	Respondents tend to present themselves in a positive light.	Thus social desirability bias is still possible.
⊖ Response bias.	Respondents may favour a particular kind of response, e.g. they always agree.	This means that all respondents tend to reply in a similar way.

Interviews

Face-to-face interaction between an interviewer and interviewee.

Structured interview – list of pre-determined questions asked in a fixed order.

⊕ Easy to **replicate**.	Straightforward to replicate because of **standardised** format.	The format also reduces differences between interviewers.
⊖ Interviewees cannot elaborate.	Interviewees cannot deviate from the topic or elaborate their points.	This may be a source of frustration for some.

Unstructured interview – there are no set questions. There is a general topic to be discussed but the interaction is free-flowing and the interviewee is encouraged to elaborate.

⊕ There is greater flexibility.	Unlike a structured interview, points can be followed up as they arise.	More likely to gain insight into interviewee's worldview.
⊖ Difficult to replicate.	Such interviews lack structure and are not standardised.	Greater risk of *interviewer bias*.

Semi-structured interviews – list of questions that have been worked out in advance but interviewers are free to ask follow-up questions when appropriate.

Design of questionnaires

Writing good questions	• Avoid jargon: Do you agree that maternal deprivation in infanthood inevitably leads to affectionless psychopathy?
	• Avoid double-barrelled questions: Do you agree that footballers are overpaid and should give 20% of their wages to charity?
	• Avoid leading questions: Do you agree that boxing is barbaric?

Closed questions – respondent has limited choices.

Data are *quantitative*, e.g. How many cigarettes do you smoke a day? 0–10, 11–20, 21–30, 30+

| ⊕ Easier to analyse. | Can produce graphs and charts for comparison. | Makes it easier to draw conclusions. |
| ⊖ Respondents are restricted. | Forced into an answer that may not be representative of true feelings. | May reduce the **validity** of the findings. |

Open questions – respondents provide their own answers expressed in words.

Data are *qualitative*, e.g. Why did you start smoking?

| ⊕ Respondents not restricted. | Answers more likely to provide detailed, unpredictable information. | Likely to have more validity than statistics. |
| ⊖ Difficult to analyse. | Wider variety of answers than produced by quantitative data. | May be forced to reduce data to statistics. |

Design of interviews

Interview schedule	A standardised list of questions that the interviewer needs to cover, can reduce interviewer bias.
Quiet room	Will increase the likelihood that the interviewee will open up.
Rapport	Begin with neutral questions to make participants feel relaxed.
Ethics	Remind interviewees that answers will be treated in confidence.

Pilot studies

Used in all types of research.

| Trial run | A pilot study is a small-scale trial run of a research design before doing the real thing. |
| Aim of piloting | To find out if certain things don't work so you can correct them before spending time and money on the real thing. |

A researcher wanted to investigate the types and severity of people's phobias. She considered using a questionnaire to collect the responses.

1. Write **one** open and **one** closed question the psychologist could use to collect her data.
   (2 marks + 2 marks)
2. Outline **one** strength and **one** limitation of using a questionnaire in this study.
   (2 marks + 2 marks)
3. The researcher decided to conduct interviews instead. Outline **two** issues she should take into account when designing the interview.
   (2 marks + 2 marks)

KNOWLEDGE CHECK

1. Explain what is meant by the term 'self-report'. *(2 marks)*
2. Explain what is meant by an 'unstructured interview'. *(2 marks)*
3. Outline **one** strength and **one** limitation of using structured interviews. *(2 marks + 2 marks)*
4. Briefly evaluate the use of questionnaires in psychological research. *(4 marks)*

Spec spotlight

Pilot studies and the aims of piloting.

KNOWLEDGE CHECK

1. Explain the purpose of using a pilot study in psychological research. *(2 marks)*

Types of data

Spec spotlight

Qualitative and quantitative data.

Primary and secondary data, including meta-analysis.

A developmental psychologist asks fathers from different cultures to describe their experiences of being a parent. The psychologist's research assistant collects data about cross-cultural child-rearing practices from online sources.

1. Explain **one** strength and **one** limitation of collecting qualitative data in this study. *(2 marks + 2 marks)*
2. Give **one** example of relevant quantitative data the psychologist could have collected. *(1 mark)*
3. Identify the primary and secondary data in this study. Explain your answer. *(4 marks)*

Primary data is sometimes called 'field research'. No, come back Ben, it's not what you think!

KNOWLEDGE CHECK

1. Referring to an example, explain what is meant by 'qualitative data'. *(2 marks)*
2. Outline **one** strength and **one** limitation of collecting secondary data in psychological research. *(2 marks + 2 marks)*
3. Referring to **one** example, briefly discuss the use of meta-analysis in psychology. *(6 marks)*

Quantitative and qualitative data

Quantitative data – *numerical data*, e.g. reaction time or number of mistakes.

⊕ Easier to analyse.	Can draw graphs and calculate averages.	Can 'eyeball' data and see patterns at a glance.
⊖ Oversimplifies behaviour.	E.g. using rating scale to express feelings.	Means that individual meanings are lost.

Qualitative data – *non-numerical* data expressed in words, e.g. extract from a diary.

⊕ Represents complexities.	More detail included, e.g. explaining your feelings.	Can also include information that is unexpected.
⊖ Less easy to analyse.	Large amount of detail is difficult to summarise.	Difficult to draw conclusions, many 'ifs and buts'.

Primary and secondary data, including meta-analysis

Primary data – 'first hand' data collected for the purpose of the investigation.

⊕ Fits the job.	Study designed to extract only the data needed.	Information is directly relevant to research aims.
⊖ Requires time and effort.	Design may involve planning and preparation.	Secondary data can be accessed within minutes.

Secondary data – collected by someone other than the person who is conducting the research, e.g. taken from journal articles, books, websites or government records.

⊕ Inexpensive.	The desired information may already exist.	Requires minimal effort making it inexpensive.
⊖ Quality may be poor.	Information may be outdated or incomplete.	Challenges the **validity** of the conclusions.

Meta-analysis – a type of secondary data that involves combining data from a large number of studies. Calculation of *effect size*.

⊕ Increases validity of conclusions.	The eventual sample size is much larger than individual samples.	Increases the extent to which **generalisations** can be made.
⊖ Publication bias.	Researchers may not select all relevant studies, leaving out negative or non-significant results.	Data may be biased because it only represents some of the data and incorrect conclusions are drawn.

Measures of central tendency

Mean – arithmetic average, add up all the scores and divide by the number of scores.

⊕ Sensitive.	Includes all the scores in the data set within the calculation.	More of an overall impression of the average than median or mode.
⊖ May be unrepresentative.	One very large or small number makes it distorted.	The median or the mode tend not to be so easily distorted.

Median – middle value, place scores in ascending order and select middle value. If there are two values in the middle, the mean of these is calculated.

⊕ Unaffected by extreme scores.	The median is only focused on the middle value.	It may be more representative of the data set as a whole.
⊖ Less sensitive than the mean.	Not all scores are included in the calculation of the median.	Extreme values may be important.

Mode – most frequent or common value, used with categorical/nominal data.

⊕ Relevant to categorical data.	When data is 'discrete', i.e. represented in categories.	Sometimes, the mode is the only appropriate measure.
⊖ An overly simple measure.	There may be many modes in a data set.	It is not a useful way of describing data when there are many modes.

Measures of dispersion

Range – the difference between highest to lowest value (+1).

⊕ Easy to calculate.	Arrange values in order and subtract largest from smallest.	Simple formula, easier than the standard deviation.
⊖ Does not account for the distribution of the scores.	The range does not indicate whether most numbers are closely grouped around the mean or spread out evenly.	The standard deviation is a much better measure of dispersion in this respect.

Standard deviation – measure of the average spread around the mean. The larger the standard deviation, the more spread out the data are.

⊕ More precise than the range.	Includes all values within the calculation.	A more accurate picture of the overall distribution of the data set.
⊖ It may be misleading.	May 'hide' some of the characteristics of the data set.	Extreme values may not be revealed, unlike with the range.

Spec spotlight

Descriptive statistics: measures of central tendency – mean, median and mode; measures of dispersion – range and standard deviation.

Apply it

A psychologist investigated the effect of chunking on the capacity of short-term memory. Participants who used chunking recalled a mean of 14.2 letters from a list, with a standard deviation of 6.7. Participants who did not use chunking recalled a mean of 7.5 letters, with a standard deviation of 1.3.

1. What conclusion can you draw from the means in this study?
   (2 marks)
2. What conclusion can you draw from the standard deviations in this study? *(2 marks)*

The number of people who support Man City or Man United in a particular class would be an example of **categorical data** *– people can only be in one category or the other.*

No, you can't be both!!

Ways of **describing** *a set of data include measures of central tendency and dispersion, and also graphs (see next spread).*

KNOWLEDGE CHECK

1. Explain what is meant by the term 'measure of central tendency'. *(2 marks)*
2. Explain how a researcher might calculate the mean. *(2 marks)*
3. Outline **one** strength and **one** limitation of standard deviation as a measure of dispersion. *(2 marks + 2 marks)*

Spec spotlight

Presentation and display of quantitative data: graphs, tables, scattergrams, bar charts.

Distributions: normal and skewed distributions; characteristics of skewed distributions.

Presentation and display of quantitative data

			SpeedUpp condition	Water conditions
Tables	Raw scores displayed in columns and rows. A summary paragraph beneath the table explains the results.	Mean	119	96
		Standard deviation	53.8	35.8

Bar chart	Categories (discrete data) are usually placed along the x axis and frequency on the y axis (or can be reversed). The height of each column represents the frequency of that item.	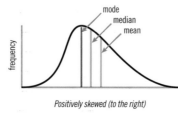

Histogram	Bars touch each other – data is continuous rather than discrete. There is a true zero.
Line graph	Frequency on one axis, data on the other axis is continuous. The line often shows how something changes, e.g. over time.
Scattergram	Used for correlational analysis. Each dot represents one pair of related data (see page 115). The data on both axes must be continuous.

A 'distribution' is a graph showing frequency data. Below is a normal distribution and two types of skewed distributions.

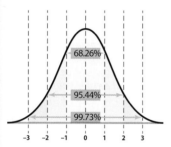

Distributions

Normal distribution – symmetrical, bell-shaped curve. Most people are in the middle area of the curve with very few at the extreme ends.

The mean, median and mode all occupy the same mid-point of the curve.

Skewed distributions – distributions that lean to one side or the other because most people are either at the lower or upper end of the distribution.

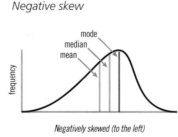

Negative skew	Most of the distribution is concentrated towards the right of the graph, resulting in a long tail on the left.
Negatively skewed (to the left)	E.g. a very easy test in which most people get high marks would produce a negative skew. The mode is the highest point of the peak, the median comes next to the left, and the mean is dragged across to the left (if scores are arranged from lowest to highest).

Positive skew	Most of the distribution is concentrated towards the left of the graph, resulting in a long tail on the right.
Positively skewed (to the right)	E.g. a very difficult test in which most people get low marks would produce a positive skew. The mode is the highest point of the peak, the median comes next to the right, and the mean is dragged across to the right (if scores are arranged from lowest to highest).

KNOWLEDGE CHECK

1. Explain what is meant by the term 'scattergram'. *(2 marks)*
2. Referring to an example, describe **two** features of a normal distribution. *(2 marks + 2 marks)*
3. Explain the difference between a normal and skewed distribution. Use an example in your answer. *(3 marks)*

Percentages	Percentage means 'divide by 100'.
Percentage to a decimal	1. Remove the % sign. 2. Move the decimal two places to the left.
Decimal to a fraction	1. Work out the number of decimal places in your number (number of digits to right of decimal point). 2. If there are two decimal places then the denominator is 100, if there are three decimal places then the denominator is 1000, etc. 3. Reduce the fraction by finding the lowest common denominator: the biggest number that divides evenly into both parts of the fraction.
Ratios	Expressed as *part-to-part ratios* or *part-to-whole ratios*. Should always be to the lowest common denominator. Example: The number of people who support Man City in a class of 20 students = 12. The number who support Man United = 8. (*I told you you couldn't be both!*) • Part-to-part ratio = 12:8 = 3:2 • Part-to-whole ratio (for City fans) = 12:20 = 3:5
Decimal places	Number of digits to the right of the decimal point. Example: 0.0045 is 4 decimal places.
Significant figures	When many numbers come after a decimal point, this may be rounded off to 1, 2 or 3 significant figures. Zeroes are not significant figures but are included as place holders. Example: The percentage chance that a Man City and Man United fan will get on well = 0.002473691* • To 1 significant figure = 0.002 (3 decimal places) • To 2 significant figures = 0.0025 • 23,450 to 2 significant figures = 23,000 (no decimal places) *not actually statistical fact – in case you were wondering.*
Standard form	A way of expressing very large or very small numbers. The formula is [number between 1 and 10] × 10$^{\text{[to the power of x]}}$. 3.2×10^5 is 320,000 (move decimal point 5 places to right) 3.2×10^{-5} is 0.000032 (move decimal point 5 places to left)

Interpreting mathematical symbols

Symbol	Symbol name	Meaning / definition	Example
=	equals sign	equality	4 = 3 + 1
>	strict inequality	greater than	3 > 2
<	strict inequality	less than	2 < 3
>>	inequality	much greater than	3000 >> 0.02
<<	inequality	much less than	0.02 << 3000
∝	proportional to	proportional to	$f(x) \propto g(x)$
≈	approximately equal	weak approximation	11 ≈ 10

KNOWLEDGE CHECK

1. Jimi indicated on a checklist of 20 compulsive behaviours that he had 14 of them. Express Jimi's score as (a) a percentage, (b) a decimal, and (c) a fraction of the total score. *(1 mark + 1 mark + 1 mark)*

2. Pi is 3.141592653, etc. Express this to three decimal places. *(1 mark)*

Statistical testing

Spec spotlight

Introduction to statistical testing: the sign test.

Table of critical values for the sign test.

Calculated value of S must be EQUAL TO or LESS THAN critical value in this table for significance to be shown.

	Level of significance for a **one-tailed test**			
	.05	.025	.01	.005
	Level of significance for a **two-tailed test**			
	.10	.05	.02	.01
N				
5	0			
6	0	0		
7	0	0	0	
8	1	0	0	0
9	1	1	0	0
10	1	1	0	0
11	2	1	1	0
12	2	2	1	1
13	3	2	1	1
14	3	2	2	1
15	3	3	2	2
16	4	3	2	2
17	4	4	3	2
18	5	4	3	3
19	5	4	4	3
20	5	5	4	3
25	7	7	6	5
30	10	9	8	7
35	12	11	10	9

Statistical testing

Significance	The difference/association between two sets of data is greater than what would occur by chance – coincidence or fluke.
	To find out if the difference/association is *significant* we need to use a *statistical test*.
Probability	Probability (p) is a numerical measure of the likelihood that certain events will occur. The accepted level of probability in psychology is 0.05 (or 5%).
	This is the level at which the researcher decides to accept the research hypothesis or not.
	If the research hypothesis is accepted, there is less than 5% probability that the results occurred by chance.
Calculated and *critical* *values*	The *calculated value* is compared with a *critical value* to decide whether the result is significant or not.
	The critical values for a particular test are given in a *table of critical values*.
Finding the critical value	To find the critical value, need to know: 1. The significance level (usually 0.05 or 5%). 2. The number of participants in the investigation (the N value) or the degrees of freedom (df). 3. Whether the hypothesis is *directional* or *non-directional*.

The sign test

Conditions of use	Used to analyse the difference in scores between related items, e.g. the same participant is tested twice.
	Can be used with nominal data (or better).
Calculation	1. The score for condition B is subtracted from condition A to produce the sign of difference (either a plus or a minus). 2. The total number of pluses and the total number of minuses should be calculated. 3. Participants who achieved the same score in condition A and condition B should be disregarded, and deducted from the N value. 4. The S value is the total of the less frequent sign.
Critical value	If S is equal to or less than critical value, then S is significant and the experimental hypothesis is retained.

KNOWLEDGE CHECK

1. Identify the **three** criteria that need to be met for a sign test to be used to analyse data.
   (3 marks)
2. Give **three** pieces of information that are needed to use a table of critical values. *(3 marks)*
3. Imagine you have calculated a sign test. Explain how you would work out whether the value of S is significant or not. *(2 marks)*

What is it?	Before publication, all aspects of the investigation are scrutinised by experts ('peers') in the field. These experts should be objective and unknown to the researcher.

Aims of peer review	• *Funding*: allocate research funding. • *Validation* of the quality and relevance of research. • *Improvements* and amendments are suggested.	

⊕ Protects quality of published research.	Minimises possibility of fraudulent research and means published research is of the highest quality.	Preserves the reputation of psychology as a science and increases the credibility and status of the subject.
⊖ May be used to criticise rival research.	A minority of reviewers may use their anonymous status to criticise rival researchers.	Often there is competition for limited research funding so this may be an issue.
⊖ Publication bias.	Tendency for editors of journals to want to publish 'headline grabbing' findings.	Means that research that does not meet this criterion is ignored or disregarded.
⊖ Ground-breaking research may be buried.	Reviewers may be much more critical of research that contradicts their own view.	Peer review may slow down the rate of change within scientific disciplines.

Spec spotlight

The role of peer review in the scientific process.

Two psychologists are carrying out longitudinal research into the effects of ageing on memory. Several participants have dropped out. One of the psychologists is tempted to make up some results, but the other warns him that this is a bad idea if they want their research to be published in a reputable journal.

With reference to this disagreement, explain why peer review is necessary in psychological research. *(4 marks)*

KNOWLEDGE CHECK

1. Explain what is meant by the term 'peer review'. *(2 marks)*
2. Outline **two** aims of peer review in psychological research. *(4 marks)*
3. Briefly discuss the use of peer review in the scientific process. *(6 marks)*

Psychology and the economy

The findings of psychological research can benefit our economic prosperity.

Attachment research into the role of the father.	• Recent research has stressed the importance of *multiple attachments* and the role of the father in healthy psychological development. • This may promote more flexible working arrangements in the family. • This means that modern parents are better equipped to contribute more effectively to the economy.
The development of treatment for mental illness.	• A third of all days off work are caused by mental disorders such as *depression*. • Psychological research into the causes and treatments of mental disorders means that patients have their condition diagnosed quickly. • Patients have access to therapies or psychotherapeutic drugs, such as SSRIs. • Sufferers can manage their condition effectively, return to work and contribute to the economy.

Spec spotlight

The implications of psychological research for the economy.

KNOWLEDGE CHECK

1. Using **two** examples, outline the implications of psychological research for the economy. *(4 marks)*

Glossary

attrition The loss of participants from a study over time, which is likely to leave a biased sample or a sample that is too small for reliable analysis. **99**

behaviourist A way of explaining behaviour in terms of what is observable and in terms of learning. **56, 70, 72–77, 85, 88, 96**

biological approach A perspective that emphasises the importance of physical processes in the body such as genetic inheritance and neural function. **70–71, 75, 78–79, 89, 104–107**

case study A research method that involves a detailed study of a single individual, institution or event. Case studies provide a rich record of human experience but are hard to generalise from. **35, 71, 85**

classical conditioning Learning by association. Occurs when two stimuli are repeatedly paired together – an unconditioned (unlearned) stimulus (UCS) and a new 'neutral' stimulus (NS). The neutral stimulus eventually produces the same response that was first produced by the unlearned stimulus alone. **56–57, 72, 96–98**

cognitive Refers to the process of thinking – knowing, perceiving, believing. **10, 22, 29, 35, 37, 41, 45–47, 66, 70–71, 73–78, 88–89, 94–95, 97, 99–103, 106**

collectivist A group of people who place more value on the 'collective' rather than on the individual, and on interdependence rather than on independence. The opposite is true of individualist culture. **13, 53, 62, 87**

confederate An individual in a study who is not a real participant and has been instructed how to behave by the researcher. **12–13, 16, 19, 26, 28**

confounding variable (CV) Any variable, other than the IV, that may have affected the DV so we cannot be sure of the true source of changes to the DV. Confounding variables vary systematically with the IV. **31, 53, 61, 63, 67, 79, 108–111**

control condition The condition in a repeated measures design that provides a baseline measure of behaviour without the experimental treatment (IV). **38**

control group In an experiment with an independent groups design, a group of participants who receive no treatment. Their behaviour acts as a baseline against which the effect of the independent variable (IV) may be measured. **26, 29, 35, 42, 49, 54, 66, 99, 108**

CR Conditioned response. In classical conditioning, the neutral stimulus (NS) becomes the conditioned stimulus (CS) after the NS has been paired with the unconditioned stimulus (UCS). The NS now takes on the properties of the UCS and produces the unconditioned response (UCR). The response is now called a conditioned response (CR). **56, 72, 96, 98**

cross-sectional One group of participants representing one section of society (e.g. young people or working-class people) is compared with participants from another group (e.g. old people or middle-class people). **53**

CS Conditioned stimulus. See CR. **56, 72, 96, 98**

demand characteristics Any cue from the researcher or from the research situation that may be interpreted by participants as revealing the purpose of the investigation. This may lead to a participant changing their behaviour within the research situation. **13, 43, 45, 108, 110, 116**

determinism The view that an individual's behaviour is shaped or controlled by internal or external forces rather than an individual's will to do something. **73, 75, 77, 79, 85, 87–89**

dopamine Neurotransmitter that generally has an excitatory effect and is associated with the sensation of pleasure. Unusually high levels are associated with schizophrenia and unusually low levels are associated with Parkinson's disease. **83, 104**

DV Dependent variable. **108–111, 115–116, 118**

EEG Electroencephalograph. A method of detecting activity in the living brain, electrodes are attached to a person's scalp to record general levels of electrical activity. **70**

experimental condition The condition in a repeated measures design containing the independent variable as distinct from the control. **75**

experimental group The group in an independent groups design containing the independent variable as distinct from the control. **109**

external validity The degree to which a research finding can be generalised to, for example, other settings (ecological validity), other groups of people (population validity) and over time (historical validity). **17, 27, 31, 33, 43, 53, 77, 110–111, 116**

extraneous variable (EV) Any variable, other than the independent variable (IV), that may have an effect on the dependent variable (DV) if it is not controlled. EVs are essentially nuisance variables that do not always vary systematically with the IV. **31, 39, 45, 108–110, 115–116**

fMRI Functional magnetic resonance imaging. A method used to scan brain activity while a person is performing a task. It enables researchers to detect those regions of the brain which are rich in oxygen and thus are active. **70, 79**

free will The notion that humans can make choices and are not determined by biological or external forces. **73, 75, 77, 85–86, 89**

generalisation In conditioning, the tendency to transfer a response from one stimulus to another which is quite similar. In relation to research findings, the extent to which findings and conclusions from a particular investigation can be broadly applied to the population. This is made possible if the sample of participants is representative of the population. **13, 17, 31, 35, 39, 55–56, 65, 67, 96, 110–113, 116, 120**

holism An argument or theory which proposes that it only makes sense to study a whole system rather than its constituent parts (which is the reductionist approach). **87, 89**

humanistic approach An approach to understanding behaviour that emphasises the importance of subjective experience and each person's capacity for self-determination. **71, 86–87, 89**

individualist A group of people who value the rights and interests of the individual. This results in a concern for independence and self-assertiveness. People tend to live in small families unlike collectivist societies. This is typical of Western cultures, in contrast to many non-Western cultures that tend to be collectivist. **13, 62, 87, 93**

informed consent An ethical issue and an ethical guideline in psychological research whereby participants must be given comprehensive information concerning the nature and purpose of the research and their role in it, in order for them to make an informed decision about whether to participate. **98–99, 110, 114**

internal validity A kind of validity, concerned with what goes on inside a study – the extent to which the researcher is measuring what was intended. In an experiment, this includes the control of variables to ensure that changes in the DV are solely due to the IV. **15, 17, 19, 53, 61, 67, 110**

IV Independent variable. **108–111, 115**

learning approach The explanation of behaviour using the principles of classical and operant conditioning. The view that all behaviour is learned, a position held by behaviourists. **71–75**

longitudinal Research conducted over a long period of time – months or years. **50, 53, 66**

meta-analysis 'Research about research', refers to the process of combining results from a number of studies on a particular topic to provide an overall view. This may involve a qualitative review of conclusions and/ or a quantitative analysis of the results producing an effect size. **47, 62–63, 120**

modelling From the observer's perspective modelling is imitating the behaviour of a role model. From the role model's perspective, modelling is the precise demonstration of a specific behaviour that may be imitated by an observer. **57, 74–75, 88**

NS Neutral stimulus. See CR. **56, 72, 96**

operant conditioning A form of learning in which behaviour is shaped and maintained by its consequences. Possible consequences of behaviour include positive reinforcement, negative reinforcement or punishment. **56, 72–73, 75, 96–97**

prefrontal cortex Section of the cerebral cortex at the front of the brain associated with working memory and planning. **35, 37, 76**

psychodynamic A perspective that describes the different forces (dynamics), most of which are unconscious, that operate on the mind and direct human behaviour and experience. **22, 71, 84–85, 89**

randomly assigned An attempt to control for participant variables in an independent groups design which ensures that each participant has the same chance of being in one condition as any other. **14–15, 17, 67**

reductionism The belief that human behaviour is best explained by breaking it down into smaller constituent parts. **77, 87–89**

replicate The opportunity to repeat an investigation under the same conditions in order to test the validity and reliability of its findings. **15, 17, 19, 41, 65, 70, 73, 110, 116, 118**

serotonin A neurotransmitter found in the central nervous system. Low levels have been linked to many different behaviours and physiological processes, including aggression, eating disorders and depression. **78, 83, 104 107**

social learning theory A way of explaining behaviour that includes both direct and indirect reinforcement, combining learning theory with the role of cognitive factors. **57, 73–75, 88**

soft determinism The concept that there are constraints on our behaviour but within these limitations we are free to make choices. **77, 88**

standardised (procedures and instructions) Using exactly the same formalised procedures and instructions for all participants in a research study. **70–71, 108, 110, 116, 118–119**

testosterone A hormone produced mainly by the testes in males, but it also occurs in females. It is associated with the development of secondary sexual characteristics in males (e.g. body hair), but has also been implicated in aggression and dominance behaviours. **75**

UCS Unconditioned stimulus. See CR. **56–57, 72, 96**

UCR Unconditioned response. See CR. **56, 72, 96**

validity Refers to whether an observed effect is a genuine one. **15, 17–19, 21, 23, 25, 27, 29, 31, 33, 35, 39, 41, 43, 45, 49, 53, 61, 63, 67, 69, 73, 77, 87, 109–111, 115–117, 119–120, 125**

Revision Guide

+

Revision App

=

An unbeatable combination for revision!

Have your cake and eat it when you combine this **Revision Guide** with its companion *Revision App*. The app content mirrors the guide but the app has special features and is ideal for revision on the go.

 Flash cards summarise all the essential knowledge

 Drill deeper for more detailed revision notes as well as exam advice

 Quizzes and challenges test and reinforce knowledge and understanding

 Web links take you to useful web pages and films

 Exam-style questions help you study and practise for the exams

 Definitions for key terms can be accessed as you read the content

Read this guide when you are at home and then consolidate your knowledge with the app when you are on the move.

Boost your revision into the stratosphere. Download the app from the Apple and Android App Stores NOW!

Visit: www.illuminatepublishing.com/psychapp for links to the app stores.